The Story of Africa
& her flags to color

Michael A. Faul, Honorary Secretary of the Flag Institute
Drawings by Nancy Conkle

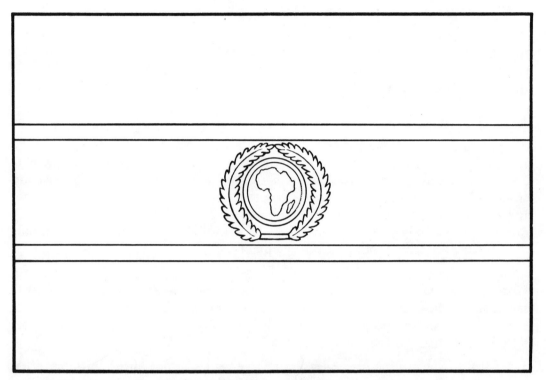

Flag of the Organization of African Unity

When the Organization of African Unity decided to adopt a flag, it quickly became clear that it would be impossible to include all the colors of the flags of Africa. The question was which colors to include, so as not to offend those countries whose colors were not shown. Nor would it have been right to choose a combination of colors which was used by a particular country, or others would be upset.

The multi-nation committee which designed the flag ignored personal, political and national jealousy. It worked on the symbolism of the flag, regardless of the colors or patterns of individual states. The result was very pleasing.

The flag is a horizontal tribar of green, white and green, with the bands separated by narrow orange stripes. In the center is a map of Africa in orange, within a green circle and an orange wreath.

The green is for the vegetation of sub-Saharan Africa. The orange is for the deserts of the north. The white is for peace and unity. It may be surprising that black is not included. The reason is that not all Africans are black (e.g. the Arabs of the north), and it was intended to avoid even the smallest suggestion of racism.

INTRODUCTION

In little over thirty years, most of Africa has passed from colonial control to independence. Beginning with Ghana in 1957, independence has been achieved by forty-four African states. Some did so by peaceful means; others needed revolution and armed conflict. These African states now form the largest bloc of countries in both the United Nations and in the Non-Aligned Movement.

On achieving independence, these states all adopted new national flags. Some recalled the conflict which had brought independence and were based on the flags of revolutionary parties which had conducted the fighting. Others simply reflected the future aspirations of the people of the country. Some showed traditional emblems from African history or culture.

There have been many changes of government in African states since independence. Some of these were by military coups. In spite of this the flags have, in general, remained the same. In only a few cases have there been alterations. Some of these have simply added, removed or altered an emblem. In a few countries entirely new designs have been adopted, but in these cases they have usually been adopted by a government which has been in power for some time. These governments believed that a new design was needed when they took a new path of political, economic and social development.

Most people in Africa would recognize the flags of the U.S.A., the U.S.S.R. and Britain without difficulty. But many would not recognize those of some O.A.U. states, even those of neighboring and sister countries. This small book is written so that Africans and people of African descent elsewhere in the world will learn to know the flags of the African states.

A word of warning is also necessary. It takes several months to prepare and publish a book, even a small book like this. So if a country should change its flag, it might be impossible to show this change in the book. Countries changing their flags usually do so without much warning. They often do not show the new design publicly until just before they begin to use it. For these reasons it is impossible for a flag-book to be completely up to date.

For the same reasons, the longer the book is in use, the more outdated it becomes. If you were to look at a flag-book published in 1957, the only African countries shown would be Egypt, Sudan, Libya, Ethiopia, Tunisia, Morocco and South Africa. Even then, the first four would be represented by flags which have long since passed out of use. For the rest there would be a few details of the flags of colonial governors and the badges used by the British colonies. This book is as up to date as it is possible to make it. If there have been changes which have occurred recently, and which are not shown here, we can only apologize.

THE PARTS OF THE FLAG

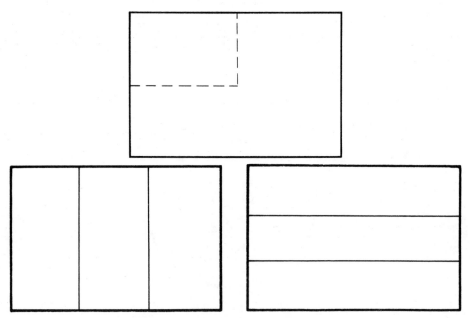

The above diagrams illustrate the terms used in the book. These terms may seem complicated at first, but they are the easiest way to describe flags.

The part of the flag nearest to the staff is called the hoist. The part of the flag furthest from the staff is called the fly. The terms began quite simply. The hoist is the part used to hoist or raise the flag, and the fly is the part which flies in the wind.

The top quarter of the flag next to the staff is known as the canton. This was used in British colonial flags to show the British Union Flag. The flag of French colonial governors showed the French flag in the canton. No African flag uses the canton as such, but several have emblems placed in that position.

A tricolor is a flag having three bands of different colors. The order of colors is given from top to bottom in a horizontally striped flag, and from the hoist to the fly in a vertically striped flag. If a flag has three stripes, but only two colors, (e.g. Nigeria), the flag is not a tricolor, but a tribar.

If a flag has an emblem placed on it, it is said to be "charged," and the emblem is a "charge."

The top corner of the flag at the staff is sometimes called the "truck point." The truck is also the name for the top of the flag-staff. The lower corner near the staff is called the "tack point." The top corner of the fly is sometimes known as the "chief point," and the bottom corner of the fly is the "base point." These terms come from the medieval art of heraldry. The old designs of coats of arms, in which many early flags originated, were shown on shields. The top of the shield was known as the chief and the bottom of the shield was the base.

At the back of the book there is a glossary of terms. These are special historical and political terms or names which are no longer familiar in everyday language. They are given with a short explanation of each. Words which appear in the glossary are italicized in the text. Each word is italicized once only, on its first appearance, not each time it appears.

ALGERIA

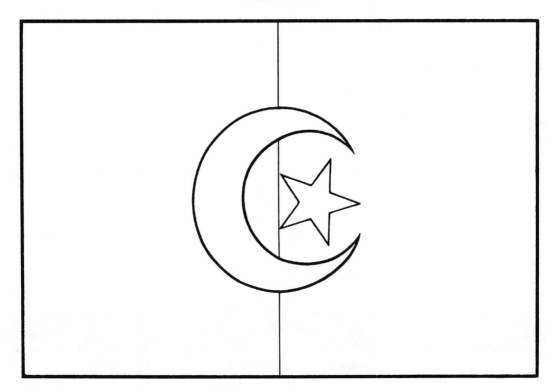

In ancient times, the coast of Algeria belonged to the *Carthaginian Empire*. Later it was controlled by the Romans. When the Roman Empire fell, the *Vandals* conquered the country. In the eighth century, Arabs came and brought the religion of *Islam*. Although there were several different groups of Arabs ruling the country at different times, it remained a *Muslim* country.

Between 1830 and 1880 Algeria was colonized from France. The Algerian people began an armed rebellion for independence in 1954. Although there had been armed risings before that date, the revolt which began in 1954 was the first nation-wide, coordinated armed struggle. Victory came in 1962 when Algeria achieved full independence.

The Algerian flag is that used during the rebellion. It is half green, at the hoist, and half white. A large red crescent appears at the join of the green and white and between the points of the crescent is a red star with one point towards the fly. It has been said the the flag was designed by Abd'el Kader, who led the fight against the French between 1832 and 1847. In fact we are not sure what flag he used. The present Algerian flag was certainly designed in 1928, and was adopted in 1958, during the armed struggle.

The crescent and star symbolize a Muslim country. The white is for peace and green was the favorite color of the Muslim Prophet, Muhammad. So the flag shows the loyalty of Algeria to Islam. Since the governments of presidents Boumedienne and Benjedid, new meanings have been given to the colors. The green is for agriculture, the white for unity, the red for socialism and the star for internationalism.

ANGOLA

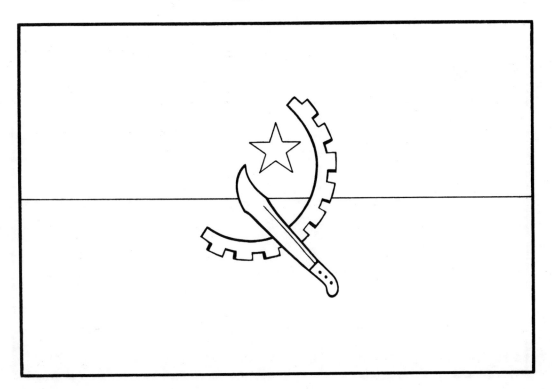

Angola is a territory of many tribes. Among the largest were the Lunda, the Bakongo, the Chokwe and the Ovimbundu. The colonization of Angola by the Portuguese began in the sixteenth century. Thus it was one of the first parts of Africa to come under European control. At first the Portuguese only occupied the coastal areas, from which they conducted the slave trade.

In the nineteenth century the Chokwe began to expand and to penetrate the territory of their neighbors. Previously they had traded with these tribes, but now they set out to conquer them. They defeated and overran the territory of the Ovimbundu, and might have created a large empire, but for the Portuguese. It was the time of the *Scramble for Africa*, and the Portuguese pushed inland from the coast and occupied all of modern Angola, including the new Chokwe empire.

Armed revolt began in Angola in 1961 and continued for fourteen years. The pro-independence forces split into three: the National Front for the Liberation of Angola (FNLA), the Popular Movement for the Liberation of Angola (MPLA) and the National Union of the Total Independence of Angola (UNITA). At independence in 1975, civil war resulted. MPLA won and became the government. FNLA was destroyed. UNITA, supported by South Africa, fought the MPLA, supported by Cuba and the USSR. In 1992 the first ever elections were held in Angola. MPLA won a majority of votes, but UNITA disputed the result, and the civil war cannot be regarded as ended.

The flag of the MPLA was halved, red over black, with a large gold star in the center. The flag of Angola is based on this. The upper half is red for the liberation struggle, and the lower half is black for the people of Angola and for Angola's identity as an African state. The flag is charged with a machete crossing half a cog-wheel and a star, all in yellow. The machete and cog-wheel are for the workers of country and town, and the star is for unity and socialism. The pattern of the emblem is based on that of the USSR.

BENIN

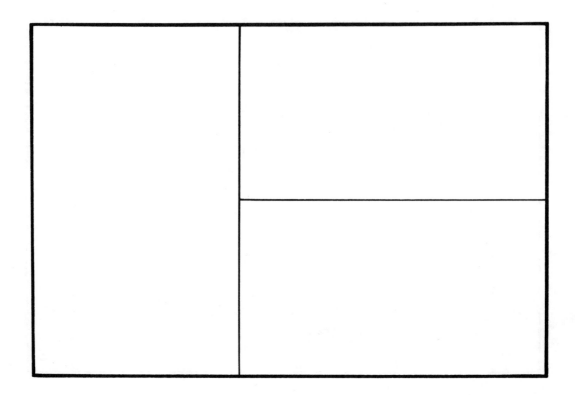

Benin was the center of an ancient civilization which extended into modern Nigeria and Togo. The people of this civilization were very advanced. Their armies were the most powerful in West Africa. There was even a regiment of women soldiers.

Benin was also famous for its bronze castings. They were of a very advanced standard, equal to anything made elsewhere in the world. Today they are very valuable, and are considered to be important art objects.

The first colonial contact was by means of the slave trade. France established *barracoons* on the coast for this purpose. She claimed Benin as a colony in 1850, but it was only in 1894 that she took full control of the country. Dahomey was the name of a kingdom which had become powerful and rich by assisting the French to obtain slaves. By this time the slave trade had long been stopped, but the name of this kingdom had replaced that of Benin. France officially named the territory Dahomey in 1911

When Dahomey achieved independence in 1960, she adopted a flag with a green vertical stripe and horizontal stripes of yellow over red. These were the colors of Ethiopia, the oldest independent African state. Many newly-independent African countries chose combinations of these colors for their flags.

Unfortunately, partly due to its many different tribes and customs, cultures and traditions, Dahomey was not stable. There were several coups and, after one of them in 1975, the new president announced that the name of the country would be changed to Benin. The name Dahomey was connected with the slave trade, while the name Benin had been used by a great African civilization. The flag was changed at the same time, but the original flag was restored in 1990.

BOTSWANA

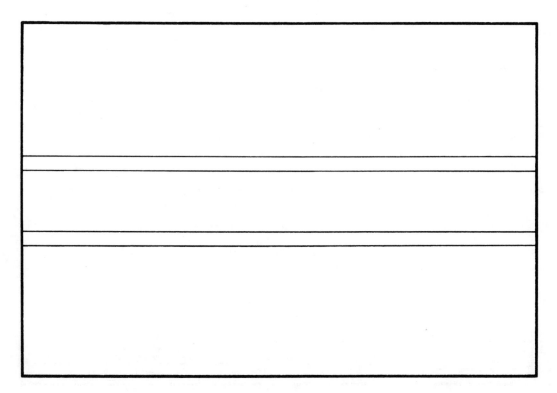

The Tswana people have lived in modern Botswana for centuries. They also lived, and some still do, in parts of South Africa. Those living in South Africa have been given "independence" in a territory known as Bophuthatswana. Only South Africa has recognized Bophuthatswana as an independent state.

The first contact the Tswana had with Europeans was in the early nineteenth century, when European missionaries came to spread the Christian religion. Later European travellers and explorers passed through the country.

In the 1880's, Chief Khama of the Bamangwato, who was effectively the leading chief of all the Tswana clans, had to make a choice. The Boers of the Transvaal and the British from the Cape both wished to annex the territory. Khama agreed with the British leader of the Cape, Cecil Rhodes, that a British *protectorate* be established. This was done in 1885. It stopped the Boers, but while the country came under British control, there was little interference with the people. The country was known as Bechuanaland Protectorate.

In 1966 the country became independent as Botswana. The first president was Sir Seretse Khama, a grandson of Chief Khama. When he died, he was succeeded by Mr. Quett Masire.

The Botswana flag is pale blue, charged with a black horizontal stripe, edged white. The black is for the majority of the people, the white for the tiny white community. Blue shows the desire for water. This is understandable, as over half the country is desert.

BURKINA FASO

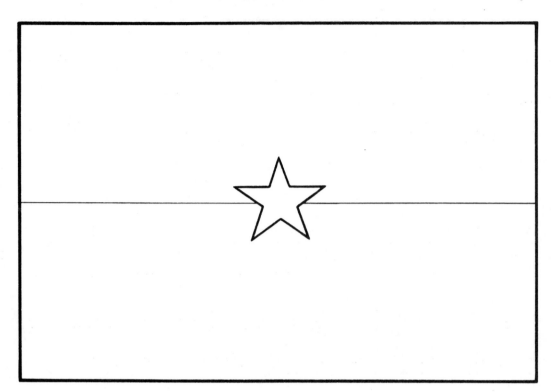

Burkina Faso was once part of the great empire of Mali. Later it broke away under a group which had immigrated into the area. These were the Mossi, and they established a kingdom which lasted for over 700 years. The Mossi are still the largest group in the population.

In 1896 the French entered the area, and in the following year they annexed it to their colony of the Ivory Coast. In 1919 it was established as the colony of Upper Volta and was included in the group of colonies known as French West Africa. Even then, there were changes, and the country several times had its frontiers altered, as parts were put under different areas to administer, or other parts were added to it. In 1947 the unity of the territory was restored, though it remained under colonial rule. The name of Upper Volta was also made permanent at that time. The name was taken from the Volta River. The country lies in the basin of the Volta River, but in the upper part, Ghana being the lower area.

Independence came in 1960. The country kept the name Upper Volta, and adopted as a flag a horizontal tricolor of black, white and red. These were for the Black, White and Red Volta rivers, which flow through the country and gave it its name, before joining into one river in Ghana.

On August 4, 1984 a new government which had seized power made two decisions. The first was to drop the colonial name of Upper Volta in favor of the more truly African name Burkina Faso. The second was to change the flag. The new flag was divided horizontally red over dark green, with a gold star in the center. The red was for the revolution and the sacrifices of the people. The green was for agriculture and prosperity. The gold star was for the natural resources of the country. The three colors together showed association with other African states which had adopted the Ethiopian colors.

BURUNDI

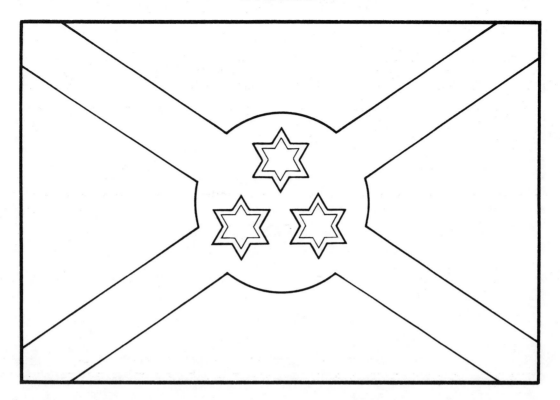

Burundi is the home of two major tribes, the Tutsi (also called Watutsi) and the Bahutu. The Tutsi average over 6 feet 6 inches in height and are the tallest people in Africa.

In the 1880's, Burundi became part of German East Africa as a result of the Scramble. After Germany lost the first World War, her colonies were taken from her by the victorious allies. Most of German East Africa was given to Britain, but Burundi and Rwanda were entrusted to Belgium as the Mandate of Ruanda-Urundi. A mandate meant that the colonial country taking control was to care for the territory until it was ready for full independence.

Independence came on July 1, 1962, when the Mandate divided into Rwanda and Burundi. At first Burundi was a kingdom and the flag, though with the same basic pattern as today, showed ancient royal emblems of a stalk of sorghum and a drum.

Burundi's first years of independence were very troubled. Of the first six prime ministers, five were assassinated. Civil war raged between the Tutsi and the Bahutu. Although he was later overthrown in a military coup, the first president, Michel Micombero, declared a republic and restored peace. That was in 1966. The following year he adopted a new flag for the country.

The basic design of the flag remained the same. The white saltire, or diagonal cross, was kept, and it stands for peace. The red quarters to the top and bottom and the green quarters to the hoist and fly were also on the royal flag. The stars in the center are red, with green edges. The red is for the sacrifices of those who fought for freedom; the green for progress and hope. The stars are for the three words of the national motto, "Unity, Peace, Progress."

CAMEROON

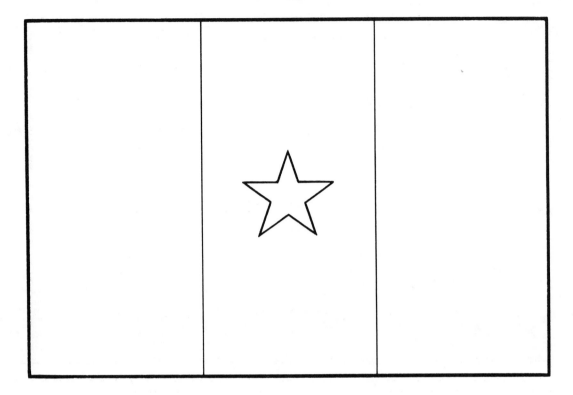

In Cameroon the people of the south are mostly Bantu in origin, while in the north there are Arabs. In the fifteenth century the Portuguese explorer, Fernão do Po, visited the coast. He found huge shoals of shrimps there. He named the area Costa dos Camerões (Coast of Shrimps). It is from this that the country takes its name.

During the centuries of the slave-trade both Portugal and Spain claimed the coastal strip, but neither of them made any real attempt to control it. In 1860, Germans began to colonize the coast. In 1884, by a treaty with some of the inland tribes, Germany established a protectorate over the southern part of the country. In 1888 she gained control of the north too. At that time Kamerun, as the Germans called the country, included parts of modern Nigeria. At the end of World War I the country was divided. France received 90% and Britain 10% of the country, both as mandates.

In 1960 the French Mandate achieved independence and adopted a flag of vertical green, red and yellow stripes. This had been designed four year previously, making Cameroon the first country to choose the Ethiopian colors for her flag. In 1961 the southern part of the British Mandate voted in a *referendum* to join Cameroon, while the northern part preferred to stay with Nigeria. The country became a federation of the original independent Cameroon and the part of the British Mandate which had voted to join it. The flag then had two small yellow stars added to the top of the green stripe.

In 1972 the federation ended and Cameroon became a united country. The basic tricolor was kept, green at the hoist, then red and yellow at the fly. The two stars were changed to a single gold star in the center for unity. Green is for hope and for the tropical jungles of the south. Yellow is for the soil of the north, for wealth and for the sun. Red is for unity and independence.

The Cape Verde Islands were colonized by the Portuguese, starting in 1462. Because of the long period under European rule and the small size of the islands, most of the people are of mixed race, known to the Portuguese as mulattoes.

In the 1960s a group known as the African Party for the Independence of Guinea and Cape Verde (P.A.I.G.C.) began an armed uprising in modern Guinea-Bissau. Although P.A.I.G.C. claimed to speak for Cape Verde, there was almost no fighting in the islands. Guinea-Bissau and Cape Verde became independent in 1974 and 1975 respectively.

The flags of the two countries were very similar, both based on the flag of the P.A.I.G.C. Each had a red vertical stripe at the hoist, charged with a black star, and each had horizontal stripes of yellow over green. The Ethiopian colors, chosen by many newly-independent African states, appear in the stripes, together with the black star of Ghana. The Cape Verde flag had other emblems added.

In 1992, a new government took control and adopted a new flag. This was quite different from any other African flag. The flag has five stripes, from the top blue, white, red, white and blue. There are ten gold stars in a circle. The blue represents the sea where the islands are situated. The red and white stripes are for the road to the future. The circle of stars shows the globe of the world and the unity of mankind, while there are ten stars for the ten islands of the country.

CENTRAL AFRICAN REPUBLIC

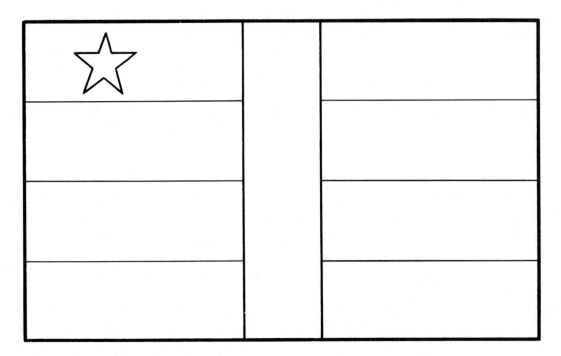

There are four tribal groups in the Central African Republic. Each has its own language, but there is also a special inter-tribal language called Sangho.

Although we do not know when the four groups arrived, some historians believe that it is in the area of the modern Central African Republic and Chad that the Bantu people originated. Certainly the four groups were there when the French arrived in 1887. The French had taken control of the lower Congo area, and were expanding inland, hoping to gain control of a band of territory right across Africa. They did not succeed in this. Eventually the territory was named Ubangui-Shari after two rivers which formed parts of the frontiers of the colony.

When the country was preparing for independence in 1958, the flag was designed by president-elect Barthélémy Boganda. It was adopted at independence in 1960. President Boganda was killed very soon afterwards in an air accident. The flag has remained unchanged, even when for a while the country was known as the Central African Empire.

The flag has a unique design. From the top the stripes are blue, white, green and yellow. The vertical stripe is red, and the star is yellow. The blue is for the rivers, the white for honesty and purity. Green is for agriculture and yellow for mineral wealth. Red is for the blood of humanity and for unity, while the star is for independence. In addition the flag has the green, yellow and red of the Ethiopian colors, showing identity with Africa, as well as the blue, white and red of France, the former colonial power.

CHAD

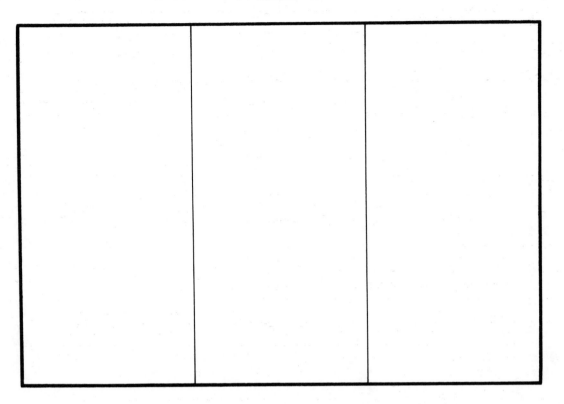

Chad and the Central African Republic may be the original home of the Bantu peoples. Caves have been found with very ancient drawings of animals and hunters, so people have lived in the area for thousands of years.

France took control of Chad in 1894 and named the territory after the large lake it shares with Nigeria. The French had made an agreement with Britain and Germany, by which Britain was to control Nigeria, Germany was to rule Cameroon and France was to take over Chad. The country remained under French control until 1960.

The government wanted to adopt the Ethiopian colors, as many of the newly independent African states were doing. Green, however, was the official color of a minority, opposition party, so blue was chosen instead. This produced a tricolor which combined the colors of France with those of Africa. The vertical stripes are blue, yellow and red from the hoist to the fly. This flag closely resembles the flag of Rumania, but this similarity is accidental.

Blue is for the sky, for hope, for agriculture and represents the south of the country. Yellow is for the sun which lights and warms the land, and represents also the deserts of the north. Red is the color of fire and stands for progress, unity and sacrifice by the people.

Unfortunately there was little national unity in Chad. Several coups occurred and there was a long and serious civil war in which outsiders like France, Libya and Zaïre were involved. More recently Chad has suffered greatly from drought and famine, and the civil war has almost stopped.

COMOROS

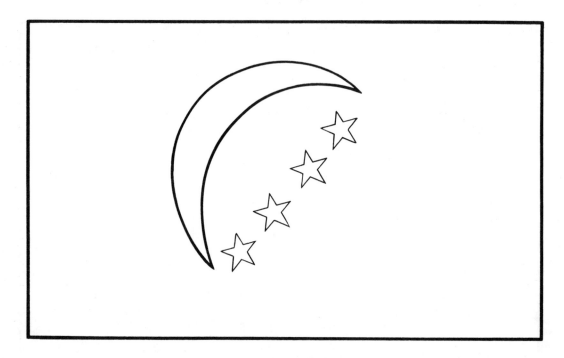

The Comoro Islands are in the Indian Ocean at the north end of the Mozambique Channel. The people are a mixture of Arabs, Bantu and Malagasy from Madagascar.

In 1841, France forced the Sultan of Mayotte to agree to allow France to control the island. In 1843, French troops landed on Mayotte. Between 1886 and 1909, France extended her control over the other islands in the group. In 1912, France established full colonial control, and placed the islands under the Sultan of Madagascar for administration.

In 1958 the people were asked if they wanted independence, but in a referendum they chose to remain part of France. In 1974 the islands voted again, this time for independence. Only the island of Mayotte preferred to stay under French rule. The islands became independent in 1975, but Mayotte still refused to separate from French control.

The flag of Comoro was officially adopted on October 1, 1978. It is based on a former flag which was used in the islands between 1963 and 1975, and which became the first flag of the independent state. The flag is green, with a crescent and four stars, all in white.

The green of the flag is for agriculture, and is also the religious color of Islam. The white crescent is also a Muslim symbol and it shows that the people of the Comoros are almost entirely Muslim by religion. The four stars are for the four main islands of the Comoros, the only four which are inhabited.

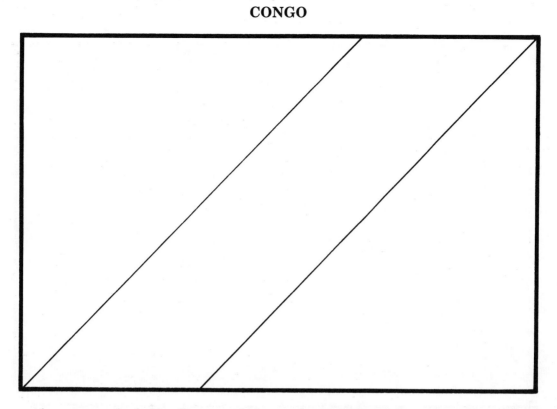

About one and a half million people live in the Republic of the Congo. The country is named for the Congo River, which in turn is named for the Bakongo people. They used to have a great civilization around the mouth of the river and extending south into modern Angola. The Bakongo still form a majority of the population, although there are other tribal groups as well.

In the eighteenth century, the coast of the country was one of the most important centers of the slave trade. After France founded Libreville in Gabon in 1849, explorers began to travel inland. In 1875, Pierre Savorgnan de Brazza began his journeys. In 1880 he signed a treaty with the chief of the Bateke tribe, who placed his people under the protection of France. In 1885, the area was named Middle Congo, and the capital city Brazzaville, named for de Brazza, was established. Brazzaville was capital not just of Middle Congo, but of French Equatorial Africa, which included also Gabon, the modern Central African Republic and Chad.

The first African governor-general of a European colony was Félix Éboué. He was a Gabonais, but he ruled French Equatorial Africa from Brazzaville. In 1944, it was in Brazzaville that the conference was held which agreed that there would be no political advancement in the French colonies. This led eventually to their independence.

For the Middle Congo, independence came in 1960, as the Republic of the Congo. A flag of diagonal stripes of green, yellow and red was chosen to show sympathy with other newly independent African countries.

In 1968 an army coup brought a new president to power. He changed the flag to a design based on that of the USSR. The flag was red, with a green wreath in the canton, surrounding a crossed hammer and hoe in yellow, with a yellow star above. The colors remained the same, but in a very different pattern. In 1991 the original flag was restored. The upper hoist triangle is green, the lower fly triangle is red. The diagonal between them is yellow. The Ethiopian colors show solidarity with other African states.

CÔTE D'IVOIRE

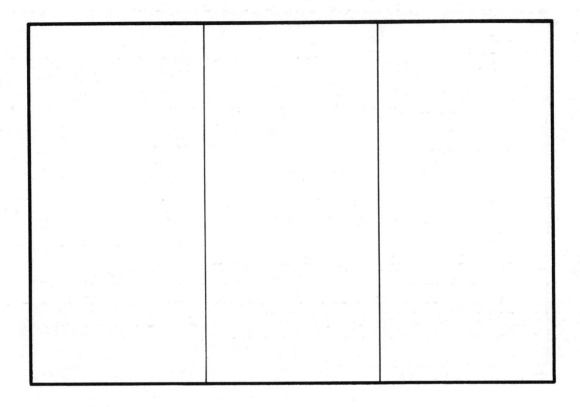

Côte d'Ivoire was formerly known in English as the Ivory Coast. The French form of the name is now official in English as well as in French.

The people of Côte d'Ivoire are a mixture of Ashanti, Agni, Baoule and Mande tribes. The earliest European contact, after the Portuguese explorers, was through the slave-trade. This continued for a very long time, but gradually ivory became more important than slaves. This is the origin of the name of the country.

In 1842 France began her influence on the coast of the country. In 1889 the area became a French protectorate, and in 1893 it was declared a French colony. The name, which had originally applied only to the coastal strip, was kept and used for the inland part of the country. The territory was then part of French West Africa.

The name was retained when the country achieved independence in August 1960. The first president was Félix Houphouet-Boigny, a former Minister of Colonies in the French government. He has remained in power ever since.

The flag was adopted on December 3, 1959, prior to independence. It is a vertical tricolor of orange, white and green, the exact reverse of the flag of the Republic of Ireland. The three stripes represent the national motto of "Union, Discipline and Work." The orange is for the sun, wealth and progress and represents the north. Green is for hope and agriculture and represents the south. White is for peace and for union between north and south. The colors can also mean the national spirit of development (orange), peace and purity (white) and hope and natural resources (green). Curiously, in the Irish flag, green represents the south, orange the north and white peace between them, just as in the flag of Côte d'Ivoire.

DJIBOUTI

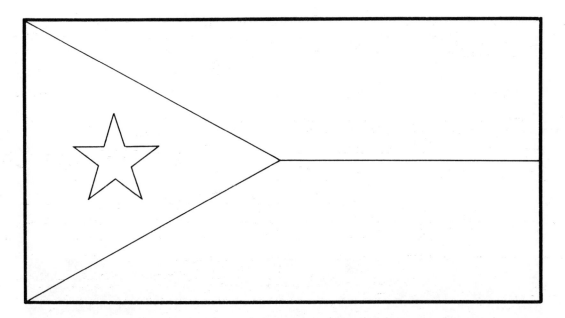

Djibouti is a small republic between Ethiopia and Somalia. The people are partly Afars (or Danakils) of Ethiopian origin, and partly Issas, who are related to the Somalis.

France began to show interest in the area as early as 1839, but it was only in 1881 that she established a permanent base there. Even then it was not until 1888 that she occupied the whole territory (small as it was) and began to build the port which today is known as Djibouti. The port was to serve as a trade outlet for Ethiopia, which at the time had no coast. It would also serve as a port of entry for France. The name of the territory was French Somaliland.

In 1967 there was a referendum on independence. The vote was in favor of remaining under French rule. One of the main reasons for this was that there was trouble then between Ethiopia and Somalia, which had affected the people of the territory. There was fear that, if independence came while the trouble continued, either Ethiopia or Somalia might try to take over the country. This would bring on more trouble, with Djibouti in the middle of it. The only change was in the name of the territory. The name French Somaliland could mean that it should belong to Somalia. The Afars were favorable to Ethiopia and did not like that idea. So the name was changed to The French Territory of the Afars and the Issas. It meant that one of the smallest countries in Africa had the longest name. In 1972 full independence was achieved under the name of Republic of Djibouti.

The flag shows horizontal stripes of light blue for the sky and sea above green for the land and agriculture. White is for peace, in the form of a triangle which is for equality. The red star is for unity. When the flag was originally designed in 1972, the blue and white were for the Issas, and refer to the flag of Somalia, while green was the traditional color of the Afars. If those meanings had been kept, the blue of the Issas would always have been higher than the green of the Afars, making the Issas seem more important. So other meanings had to be found if there was to be peace between the communities.

EGYPT

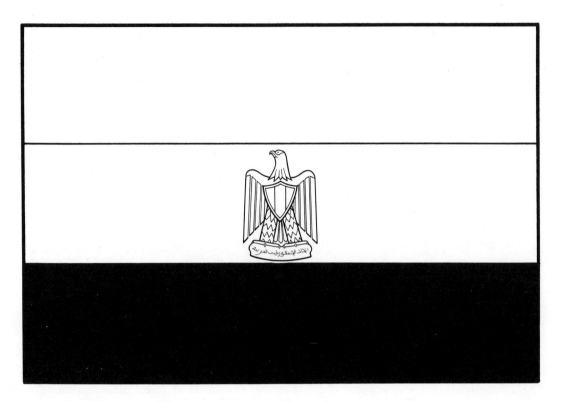

Ancient Egypt had one of the most wonderful and lasting of the old civilizations. It lasted for 3500 years, almost unchanged. Egypt fell under the control of the Greeks in the fourth century B.C. and, then not long before the birth of Christ, under the Roman Empire. In the seventh century A.D. the country was captured by the Muslim Arabs and has been a Muslim and Arab state ever since.

There have been many rulers of Egypt since the Muslim conquest, most of them foreign, like Saladin, the great *Kurdish* soldier and statesman and Shajar-ad-Durr (Spray of Pearls), the *Circassian* queen. Even Mehemet Ali, who tried to establish Egyptian independence in the nineteenth century, was an Albanian.

Britain took control of Egypt in 1882, when the Egyptian government became bankrupt. She restored Egyptian independence in 1922, but kept troops there to protect the Suez Canal. The British left in 1956, only to return the same year as a result of the Suez War between Israel and Egypt. The then president of Egypt, Gamal Abd-el Nasser, was for a long time the effective leader and spokesman of the Arab world.

Egypt's flag at independence was green with a white crescent and three white stars, for a Muslim country. When Egypt joined with Syria, forming the United Arab Republic in 1958, a new flag was adopted. It was a horizontal tricolor of red over white over black, with two green stars on the white. This is now the flag of Syria. The colors are the Arab nationalist colors and appear on the flags of many Arab nations.

The union broke up in 1961 and later Egypt replaced the stars with her national emblem in gold. Red is for the revolution which established the republic in 1952. White is for peace and prosperity. Black is for the dark past. The national emblem is the eagle of Saladin, which has been used as a national emblem in Egypt for nearly 700 years. On the eagle's chest is a shield in the form of the national flag. Thus the old and the new are combined in a single symbol.

EQUATORIAL GUINEA

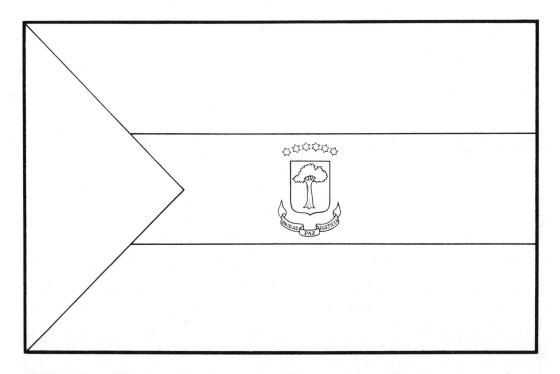

Equatorial Guinea consists of six parts, a mainland area called Río Muni, and five islands. The capital is Malabo on the island of Bioko. Before they came under European control, these were all entirely separate areas.

In 1472, the Portuguese explorer, Fernão do Po, was the first European to visit the area. Later the island of Bioko was named after him. Soon after, the Portuguese established a base for the slave-trade on Bioko. This lasted until 1778, when the islands were ceded to Spain. The mainland area was occupied by Spain later. Under Spanish rule, the territory was known as Spanish Guinea.

On October 12, 1968 the country became independent under its present name. The first president was Macias Nguema. Not long after independence he renamed the island of Bioko after himself. Although he was of the Fang tribe, from the mainland, he based his rule on the island. He antagonized the Bubi tribe of the island and proved so bad a ruler that almost a third of the population went into exile in Gabon, Cameroon or Nigeria. Later he was overthrown in a coup.

The country has retained the flag it had at independence. It is a horizontal tricolor of green, white and red, with a blue triangle at the hoist. Green is for natural resources, white for peace and red for the independence struggle. The blue triangle is for the sea, which joins the mainland and island parts of the country.

At independence the flag did not bear the *coat of arms* on the white stripe. This was added soon afterwards. The coat of arms shows a silk-cotton tree, with green foliage and a brown trunk on a silver shield. Above are six gold stars for the mainland portion of the country and the five islands. Below is the motto: "Unity, Peace, Justice" in black on a white scroll. The flag should officially have the coat of arms but is often seen without it. This is because it is difficult and more expensive to make a flag showing the arms than to have a plain white stripe.

ETHIOPIA

Ethiopia is the oldest independent state in Africa. In ancient times it was known as Axum, but the name Ethiopia occurs as early as the Bible. It did not always have its present frontiers.

The heart of Ethiopia is the land of the Amhara. During the late nineteenth century, the emperors Theodore and Menelik expanded the country, taking control of areas such as Wollo, Tigre, Choa and the Ogaden. In 1896, the Italians tried to take over Abyssinia (as Ethiopia was known for a while). They were defeated at Adowa. So Ethiopia was the only African country to preserve its independence against a European invasion. In 1935-36 Italy conquered Ethiopia. Resistance to Italy continued and in 1941, during World War II, the Ethiopians helped Allied forces to drive out the Italians.

Ethiopia was restored and, in 1952, she gained the former Italian colony of Eritrea. In 1974 a coup overthrew Emperor Haile Selassie and established a republic. In 1977, President Mengistu began to transform Ethiopia into a socialist state. He was ousted in 1991. At the same time, forces seeking independence for Eritrea and Tigre won victories over the Ethiopian army. These events may lead to the loss of the provinces and the creation of two more African states.

The flag of Ethiopia was originally three separate pennants of green, yellow and red, flown on the same staff, in no particular order. The flag was established on October 6, 1897, with red on top. This was soon changed to the present order of green over yellow over red.

There have been several explanations of the meaning of the colors. Religiously green is for the Holy Spirit and hope, yellow is for Christ and charity, red is for God the Father and faith. They can also represent the areas of the country: green—Choa, yellow—Amhara, red—Tigre. The present government has given new meanings to the colors. Green is for agriculture, yellow for minerals and red for people. Between 1957 and 1963 when many African states achieved independence, a number of them chose flags in the Ethiopian colors. This was to show respect for and solidarity with the oldest independent African country.

GABON

Gabon was once the principal center of the Pygmy peoples. The arrival of the Bantu pushed the Pygmies into the north-east of the country.

The first European to see the country was the Portuguese explorer, Diogo Cão, in 1484. Throughout the sixteenth and seventeenth centuries several trading posts were established by the French, British and Dutch on the coast. Some of these were for the slave-trade, but most were for other types of commerce. Most of them were short-lived, as the climate was unhealthy for Europeans. As soon as one group left, however, another would arrive, so trade was continuous.

In 1839 Gabon became a French protectorate. It was the third French-controlled territory in Africa after Senegal and Algeria. In 1910 Gabon was joined with Congo, Chad and the modern Central African Republic in French Equatorial Africa. Félix Éboué, the first black governor-general of a French colonial territory, was a Gabonais. In 1940, when France was defeated and occupied by Nazi Germany, only a few Frenchmen wanted to continue the fight alongside General de Gaulle, the resistance leader. Éboué brought French Equatorial Africa onto de Gaulle's side. From the colony, Free French troops crossed the Sahara and took part in the liberation of Europe.

Gabon achieved independence on August 17, 1960. Since then it has proved to be one of the most stable African states. There has been neither civil war, nor a single coup.

The flag was adopted at independence and has remained unchanged. A horizontal tricolor of green over yellow over blue, it is based on a former flag, also of green, yellow and blue, but with the French tricolor in the canton. Green is for the forests which are the greatest natural resource in the country. Yellow is for the sun and the Equator which crosses Gabon. Blue is for the sea. Some Gabonais like to think of the yellow as being the sandy beaches. So in this case the flag shows the sea, with the yellow beaches and the green forest above.

GAMBIA

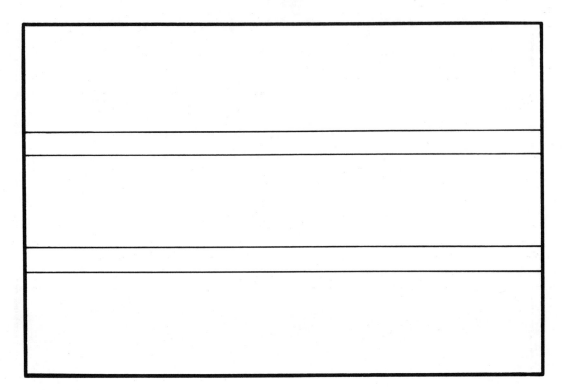

The Gambia was once part of the ancient empire of Ghana. Later it was also part of the empire of Mali.

Europeans first visited the area in the fifteenth century, when Portuguese explorers passed by. Soon afterwards, British slave-trading bases were established, and the territory became one of the major centers of the trade.

In 1783 Britain took full control of the mouth of the Gambia river. When the slave trade was abolished and outlawed in 1807, this area was one of the bases from which the British tried to suppress the trade. For a while it was placed under control of a British governor in Sierra Leone, but in 1888 it became a separate colony.

On February 18, 1965 the Gambia became independent, and in 1970 the constitution was changed so that the country became a republic. The flag was adopted at independence and has remained unchanged.

The blue stripe in the center is for the Gambia River, which flows through the entire country from east to west, and from which the country takes its name. The red stripe above represents the sun, and the green stripe below is for agriculture. The narrow white stripes which separate the other colors are for unity and peace. The design also shows the river dividing the two parts of the country, yet also uniting them.

In 1982 there was an attempted coup. It was put down by soldiers from neighboring Senegal. The two countries agreed to a federation called Senegambia. This made no difference to the flags of either country, and the federation never really became effective.

GHANA

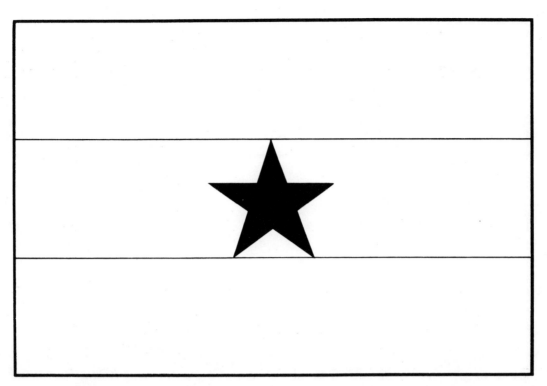

Some eighty tribes live in Ghana, the largest of which is the Ashanti. The name of the country is taken from the ancient empire, though modern Ghana does not contain any territory from that empire.

European contact began in 1470 with the arrival of Portuguese explorers. The Portuguese established a trading base, but were driven out by the Dutch. In turn the Dutch were challenged by British, French and Danish traders. This trade was for two main items, gold and slaves. The name given to the area by the Europeans was the Gold Coast. Inland, the Ashanti soon realized that wealth could be made in the slave-trade. They had traded slaves with Arab slavers to the north for centuries. Now the Europeans offered better trade-goods, and the trade prospered.

By 1871 the British had complete control of the coast. By 1901 almost the whole country was under British control as the colony of the Gold Coast. The only addition was in 1919, when part of the former German colony of Togoland was added under a British mandate.

On March 6, 1957, the Gold Coast became independent as Ghana. Although the country contained no territory of the ancient empire, the name was chosen to commemorate Africa's past greatness. In 1960 Ghana became a republic.

The flag is the reverse of that of Ethiopia, red over yellow over green, with the addition of a black star. Red is for those who fought for freedom, yellow for the country's wealth. Green is for forests and farms, while the black star is the lodestar of African freedom. Following Ghana's example, many newly-independent African states chose combinations of the Ethiopian colors, with or without the addition of Ghana's black. In 1964 the flag was changed. The yellow stripe was made white, to follow the colors of the ruling party. After the overthrow of President Kwame Nkrumah in 1966, the flag was changed back to its original pattern. Curiously, Nkrumah had designed the original flag, and then made the change.

GUINEA

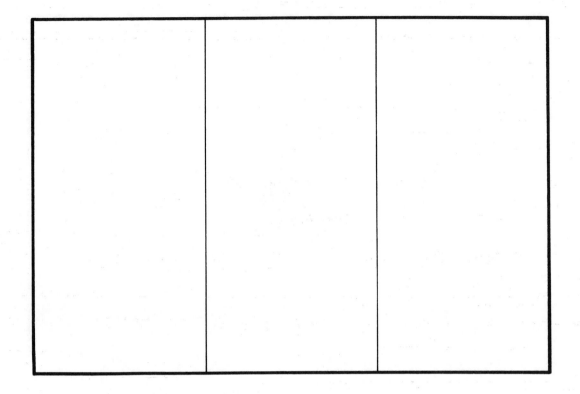

In the fourteenth century a Spanish priest who had travelled widely wrote: "The King of Guinea has a gold flag with a black mountain in the middle." The priest did not reach West Africa and Africans did not use flags then, so what he wrote cannot be correct. It does show two things. Flags were considered important enough, even then, to be mentioned as emblems of power in countries, and the name of Guinea was known in Europe 600 years ago. The name was not used by the modern country then, but meant any part of "black" Africa.

The three main tribes of Guinea are the Baza, the Fulani and the Malinké. Samori, the great military leader who resisted the French in the nineteenth century, was a Fulani and based his campaign in modern Guinea.

Guinea finally fell under French control in 1882 and became part of French West Africa. It remained so until 1958. In that year, France adopted a new constitution. The French colonies were allowed to vote on this, but were told that any who voted against it would be given independence and cut off from French aid. Only Guinea, led by Sekou Touré, voted against the constitution. Guinea was given independence and Touré became the first president. He remained president until his death.

The flag of Guinea is a vertical tricolor of red, yellow and green. The colors are those of Ethiopia. The pattern is that of the French flag, though this may be only because of the need to have a pattern different from those of Ethiopia and Ghana. Red is for the blood shed for freedom (though this refers to the time of Samori, rather than to 1958). Yellow is for the sun and for mineral wealth. Green is for the country's vegetation and agriculture. The colors also stand for the three parts of the national motto, red for labor, yellow for justice and green for solidarity. The flag is also the exact reverse of the flag of Mali.

The main tribal groups in Guinea-Bissau are the Fulani, Mandingo, Balante and Papel. These groups often exist in neighboring Senegal and Guinea too.

The Portuguese claimed control of the territory as early as 1446 and used the coast as a base for the slave trade. In 1870 Britain, which had been disputing ownership, agreed to Portuguese control, and in 1886, an agreement with France established the country's modern frontiers.

In 1959 came the first demand for independence. In 1960 rebellion began. It was led by the African Party for the Independence of Guinea and Cape Verde (P.A.I.G.C.). Most of the fighting occurred in Guinea-Bissau, very little if any in the Cape Verde Islands. The fighting was very bitter. Of the population of the territory, about one sixth fled as refugees to neighboring countries.

Guinea-Bissau had been one of the first of Portugal's colonies. It was also the first in Africa to gain independence, in 1974. The new nation had a problem over which name to adopt. The colonial name of Portuguese Guinea could not be used, and Guinea by itself would cause confusion with the neighboring state. It was decided to add the name of the country's capital city, to make the name Guinea-Bissau.

The country adopted as its flag the design used by the P.A.I.G.C. during the war. The red vertical is for the armed struggle. Yellow for work and for crops is above green for natural resources and hope for the future. The black star represents the people. The P.A.I.G.C. flag did not have the star, but the initials of the party in black on the red vertical. P.A.I.G.C. was also involved in Cape Verde, so it is not surprising that the original flag of Cape Verde was very similar to that of Guinea-Bissau.

KENYA

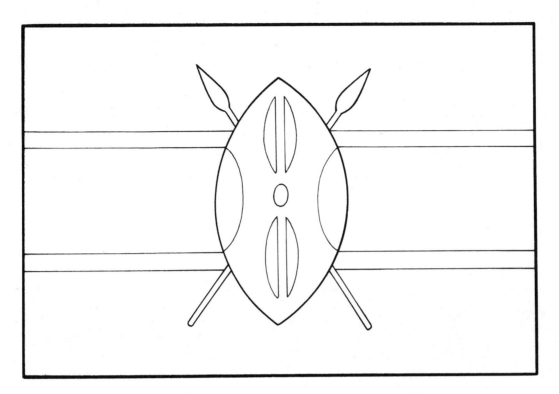

Kenya has about 19 million inhabitants. There are many African tribes among them, as well as Arabs, Indians and Europeans, so Kenya is a fully multiracial state.

Europeans first came to Kenya to trade in 1887. At that time the coast was ruled by the Sultan of Zanzibar. There had been Arab slave-traders in the area for hundreds of years. In 1895 Britain established a protectorate over Zanzibar, including the Kenya coast. From there the British linked up with the existing protectorate of Uganda. At first the combined territory was known as Ibea, which was short for Imperial British East Africa. Later the British separated them and they took their modern names. Kenya was named for Mount Kenya, the highest mountain in the country, sacred to the Kikuyu people.

Kenya was the scene of one of the early liberation wars, the Mau Mau rebellion. It was not successful and British troops quickly put most of it down. It never died out completely. In 1963, when Kenya became independent, Jomo Kenyatta, whom the British had convicted of organizing Mau Mau, became prime minister. Later he was the first president when the country became a republic. He led the Kenya African National Union (K.A.N.U.), originally a tribal party, which he made into a national force. Kenya has proved a very stable country. Many feared that trouble would occur when Kenyatta died. It did not. Daniel arap Moi became president without fuss.

The flag has a black stripe for the majority of the people over a red stripe for the struggle for independence and a dark green stripe for agriculture. The narrow white stripes represent non-African minorities. In the center is a traditional African shield and weapons. The shield is red, with black curves at the sides and white center decoration and weapons. This is based on the shields of the Masai people. They were against the Mau Mau and opposed Kenyatta. So this showed reconciliation between former opponents.

Lesotho began as a country of refugees. Early in the nineteenth century there were serious wars among the Basotho peoples of South Africa. These were made far worse by invasions and raids carried out by the neighboring Nguni tribes, like the Zulu and the Swazi. The result was that whole tribes of the Sotho were wiped out and lost their identity.

Then Moshesh gathered the remains of these tribes and moved to the mountainous area of modern Lesotho. From his headquarters at Thaba Bosiu, Moshesh defeated the Zulus, the Boers, and the British in turn. In 1868, fearing further attacks from the Boers, Moshesh asked for British protection. The territory became the British protectorate of Basutoland.

The country is completely surrounded by South Africa. Before Lesotho achieved independence in 1966, there had been several suggestions that she should simply become part of South Africa. The people of the country strongly resisted such suggestions. On October 4, 1966, the country became independent under the name of Lesotho. It is still surrounded by South Africa, and this makes it difficult for the country to have an independent life.

The first flag of Lesotho showed a traditional straw hat on a blue background, with red and green stripes at the hoist. The present flag is quite different. It is a diagonal tricolor of white over light blue over green. The white is for peace. The blue stripe is for the sky and for rain. The green is for the land. In the white appears the brown outline of the Lesotho coat of arms. It is a Sotho shield with its carry-stick behind, and a crossed club and spear. When seen in full, the shield has a crocodile on it, the emblem of the BaKwena people, of whom Moshesh was one.

LIBERIA

Liberia is unique in that it is the result of colonization by black Americans. In 1816 the American Colonization Society was founded. It was authorized by the U.S. Congress to send to West Africa those freed black slaves who chose to leave the United States. The first group of former slaves arrived in 1822. The experiment was not successful. Most slaves had been born in America and knew no other country. Africa was as foreign to them as it was to white Americans.

In 1847, the 3000 ex-slaves who had arrived declared a republic called Liberia. The name means Land of Freedom. The capital was named Monrovia after President Monroe of the United States, who had helped the Colonization Society. In 1857 it united with a smaller republic called Maryland, which recognized Liberia, as did other major countries, but its final frontiers were not decided until the 1890s. Liberia is the second oldest independent state in Africa after Ethiopia.

The flag shows Liberia's American origins. It is based on the flag of the United States. There are six red and five white stripes with a blue canton and a white star. The stripes are for the eleven men who signed the Liberian Declaration of Independence. The single star is for the country itself, a bright light of freedom in what was the "Dark Continent." Red is for courage and to commemorate the founders of the country. White (stripes) is for purity. White (star) is for freedom. Blue is for the "Dark Continent" of Africa. It may seem odd that an African state should refer to Africa as "dark." It should be remembered that little was known of Africa when Liberia was founded. As Ethiopia was hardly known, it did seem that Liberia was the only sovereign, independent state in black Africa.

After a long period of stability, Liberia sadly plunged into civil war in 1991. The president was killed and two anti-government forces defeated the Liberian army. Then the two forces began to fight each other. A peace-keeping force sent by other West African countries has been unable to stop the fighting.

LIBYA

Libya, like Egypt, was inhabited by highly civilized people from very early times. Traces of Egyptian, Greek and Roman civilizations are found throughout the country. In the seventh century, Libya was conquered by the Arabs and became part of the Muslim empire. In the mid-sixteenth century, Libya came under the control of the Ottoman Turks, who were also Muslim.

In 1911-12, Italy was at war with Turkey. Turkey was defeated and had to give control of Libya to Italy. The Arab peoples of Libya resisted the Italians, and the country only came fully under Italian rule when, in 1931, the resistance leader, Omar el Mukhtar, was executed.

In 1951 Libya became independent, the first African state to do so after World War II. It was a kingdom and used a flag based on a design which dated from before independence. It had a broad black stripe with a white crescent and star, between a narrow upper red stripe and a narrow lower green stripe. In 1969 a revolution overthrew the king and established a republic. The flag was changed to one of red, white and black stripes, showing solidarity with other Arab states which had flags of this basic pattern. In 1971, Libya joined the Federation of Arab Republics, with Egypt and Syria. There was a further change in the flag. All three countries agreed to show the same emblem in the center of their flags. Thus all three flags were identical, having the pattern used by Egypt today.

The Federation broke up in 1977, over Egypt's peace treaty with Israel. Libya not only left the Federation, but refused to continue using a flag which even resembled that of Egypt. The present flag is plain green. There are two reasons for this. It refers to the "Green Revolution" in which Libya is using money from its oil exports to develop agriculture in areas which were once entirely desert. The other reason is that the president of Libya has said that all other colors are offensive to some people, but green offends no one.

MADAGASCAR

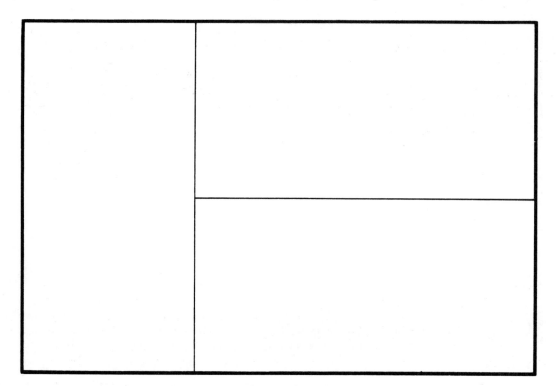

The Democratic Republic of Madagascar is the official name for the island of Madagascar, off the east coast of Africa. The population is a mixture of African peoples with Arabs, Malaysians and Polynesian peoples from the east. So the people are unique to Africa and form a distinct group known as the Malagasy.

In the seventeenth century, the French established some trading posts in the north of the island. They were prevented from gaining any real control by the power of the Hova. These were a group of wealthy landowners. They provided the kings, other rulers and military leaders of the island.

In the nineteenth century, Britain began to show interest and competed with France for influence in Madagascar. In 1885, Queen Ranavalona III agreed to a French protectorate. Then in 1896, France declared the island a colony. This brought about a massive popular revolt. 100,000 people died before it ended in 1905. France kept control. After World War II, another rebellion occurred in 1947, with a similar death-toll.

In 1956 France granted self-government to the island. Independence was achieved on June 26, 1960. Two years earlier, the flag had already been approved. It was chosen as the result of a competition. The colors were partly based on the family colors of the Hova. At the hoist is a white vertical panel. The remainder is divided red over green.

Red was the color associated with the Volemana family. White was the color of the Volafotsi family. Both families had been leaders of the revolts of 1896 and 1947. But the Hova had been based entirely in the interior of Madagascar, so green was chosen to represent the coastal peoples. The pattern of the flag is taken from old Hova flags from before the period of colonization. To ensure that there is no jealousy between the various groups, new meanings have been given to old colors. White is for purity, red for independence and green for hope.

MALAWI

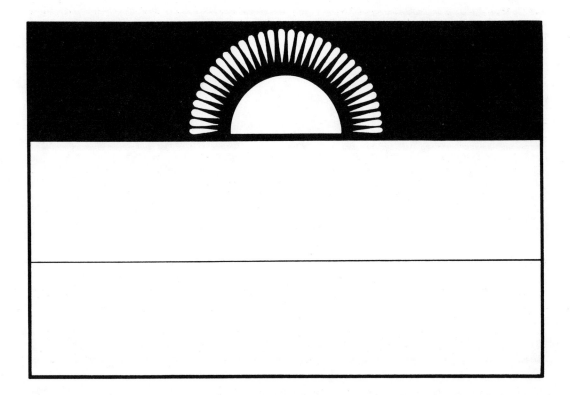

In the 1830's the Angoni settled in modern Malawi and joined the Chichewa people who were already there. Both groups suffered greatly from the Arab slave-trade. In 1859, the Christian missionary, doctor and explorer, David Livingstone, visited the territory. He later, in Britain, published an account of the evils of the trade. Partly as a result of Livingstone's book, Christian missionaries entered the country. They hoped to spread the Word of God and also to stop, or at least reduce, the damage and suffering caused by the slave-trade.

Thirty years later, there were still slave-raids taking place. It was also the time of the Scramble for Africa. The missionaries asked the British government to establish a protectorate over the area, in order to end the slave-trade completely. The British government agreed, partly because of what the missionaries said, and partly to prevent Portugal or Germany from gaining control of the area. The country remained under British rule after that, under the name of Nyasaland. In 1953 it was joined with Southern Rhodesia (now Zimbabwe) and Northern Rhodesia (now Zambia) in a federation.

Most Malawians opposed federation. When it was dissolved in 1963, the Malawi Congress Party became the government. In March 1964, Malawi became independent. The first prime minister was Dr. Hastings Kamuzu Banda. He later became the first president when Malawi changed to a republic. He has ruled Malawi ever since.

During the campaign against federation and for independence, the Malawi Congress Party used a horizontal tricolor of black over red over green. When the country achieved independence, this became the national flag, with the addition of a red sun with 32 rays. Green is for the land and its vegetation, red is for the blood shed for freedom, black is for the people of Africa, among whom rises the sun of hope for freedom and prosperity in future.

MALI

After the ancient empire of Ghana collapsed, a new empire called Mali grew up, covering most of the territory of the modern republic. The new empire was based on the Malinke people, and lasted from the late eleventh to the early seventeenth century, a little over 500 years. By the time the empire came into existence, the area had been under strong Muslim influence for a long time.

In the 1850's the French began to penetrate the area. In 1879 their first military invasion occurred. Then in 1892, France began to colonize the country. Samori, the resistance fighter, operated from Guinea into southern Mali. His resistance only served to anger the French. In 1898 they sent a large army which defeated Samori and occupied the whole country. They then named the country French Sudan and linked it with other colonies in French West Africa.

In the 1950's Modibo Keita became a major political figure. He approved of the French referendum of 1958, which Guinea rejected. Then he began to work for a negotiated independence, which would not cut the country off from French aid. In 1959, French Sudan joined with Senegal in the Federation of Mali. It lasted only a few months. When it broke up, the two territories gained separate independence. French Sudan adopted the name of the ancient empire of Mali.

The flag of the Mali Federation was a vertical tricolor of green, yellow and red, the Ethiopian colors. When the federation broke up, Senegal kept the flag with the addition of a green star in the center. Mali too kept the flag, but added the black figure of an African dancer (the kanaga) on the yellow stripe. The addition of black complimented Ghana, just as the flag's basic pattern complimented Ethiopia and Guinea, and showed Mali's solidarity with both. Less than a year later the kanaga was removed, due to Muslim pressure. Islam does not permit any pictures of human beings.

Now Mali has the flag of the federation again. Green is for agriculture, yellow for purity and natural resources, red for the blood shed for freedom at the time of Samori.

MAURITANIA

Mauritania was originally inhabited by a people known as Berbers. They came into contact with Arabs who converted them to Islam. Most of today's Mauritanians are descended from the Almoravids, a division of Islam which arose in Morocco, but which affected all of north-west Africa. The Almoravids broke up into tribes which remained independent until the French took control of the territory in the nineteenth century.

As early as 1448 the Portuguese built a fort at Arguin on the coast of modern Mauritania. In later centuries, not only Portuguese, but Dutch, British, Spanish and French came to the coast to trade. At the end of the eighteenth century, the French signed a trade treaty with the kingdom of Trarza, in the interior of the country. This gave them a great advantage over the other countries.

In the 1890's the French took full control of the country. It was included in French West Africa. There was continuous resistance to the French, but it was on a tribal rather than a national scale. Because it was not united, the French were able to overcome the resistance with ease.

On November 28, 1960, Mauritania achieved independence and adopted as her national flag a design first proposed two years earlier. The design is simple and dignified, but full of meaning. The green field is the color of Islam and of hope. In addition it shows the need for crops in this semi-desert country. The crescent and star are also Muslim. They too show loyalty to the religion of Islam. Both point upwards towards heaven, and show the need to strive continually for improvement. They are gold for mineral resources and wealth.

After 1975, with the partition of Western Sahara between Mauritania and Morocco, Mauritania became involved in war with the Polisario Front, which was supported by Algeria. In 1979 Mauritania withdrew from the war and from the Western Sahara.

MAURITIUS

Mauritius is an island 530 miles east of Madagascar in the Indian Ocean. The first Europeans to visit the island were the Portuguese explorers. In 1505 Pedro de Mascarenhas arrived on the coast, but he did not take possession of it for Portugal. In 1598, the Dutch, led by van der Neck, took control for Maurice of Nassau, the Prince of Holland. They also named the island for the Prince. The reason for the Dutch occupation was to exploit the forests of ebony on the island. They abandoned the island in 1710.

Two years later the French arrived and began to colonize Mauritius. Due to this colonization, there is a very strong French influence among the people of the island. During the Napoleonic War, British troops occupied Mauritius in 1810. In the treaty which ended the war, Mauritius was given to Britain. The British introduced sugar as a major cash crop and imported Indian laborers to work the plantations. Later Chinese were also brought in for the same purpose. This helps to explain the rich cultural variety of modern Mauritius.

After 158 years of British rule, Mauritius became independent on March 12, 1968. As a national flag she chose a simple design of four horizontal stripes, red over blue over yellow over green. Red is for the blood shed for independence, blue for the waters of the Indian Ocean which surround the island. Yellow is for freedom and independence and green is for the fertility of the land and for agriculture.

MOROCCO

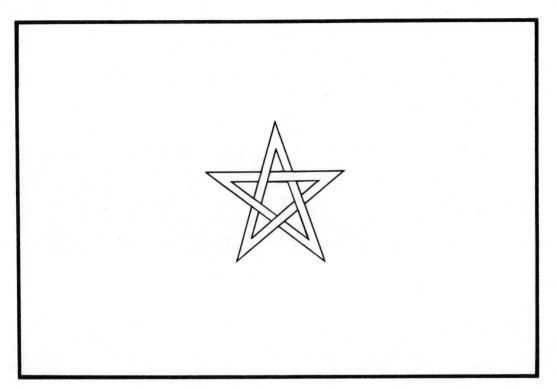

Morocco was once part of the Carthaginian Empire, then of the Roman Empire. It came in turn under the rule of the Vandal invaders, the *Byzantine Empire* and then the Muslim Arabs. The Moroccans were fiercely independent and soon gained their freedom, while remaining faithful to Islam. Morocco became the center of two great Muslim empires, those of the Almoravids and the Almohads.

Between 1880 and 1908, France gradually increased her influence in Morocco. In 1908 she intervened to put a puppet Sultan on the throne of the country, after first expelling the rightful ruler, Abd el-Aziz. Until then the Moroccans had accepted French influence, without liking it. This action provoked an armed rebellion in 1911, to overthrow the French puppet and restore the rightful ruler. After some very serious fighting and many deaths on both sides, the rebellion failed. France remained in control, in spite of later, smaller risings, until 1956.

On March 2, 1956, France gave independence to Morocco. A month later, Spain returned to Morocco some small areas which she had taken over during the Scramble. In 1957, after some discussion on what form of government the country should have, Morocco was proclaimed a kingdom.

Before colonization, and during the rebellions, the flag of Morocco had been plain red. This could have led to confusion with some other flags, notably those of Oman in Arabia and Zanzibar in East Africa. To avoid confusion, the French puppet Sultan had added a green five-pointed star to the flag. Under French rule, this star had been used unofficially in yellow, on a red flag, with the French tricolor in the canton. When Morocco became independent, the red flag with the green star was adopted as the national flag.

The red background to the flag is that of the old Moroccan flag. The green star is for Islam.

MOZAMBIQUE

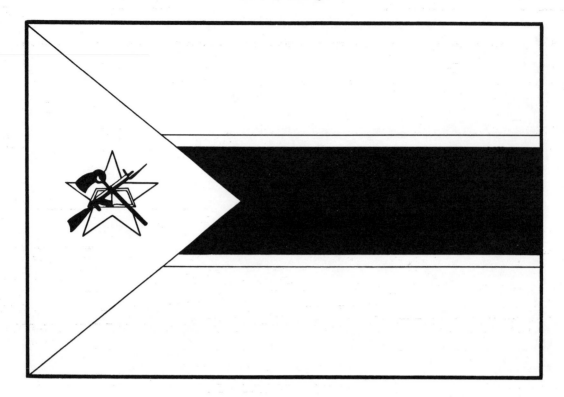

Large parts of central Mozambique were included in the ancient empire of Mwenemutapa, along with most of modern Zimbabwe. Many Mozambicans speak a language related to that of the Shona people who form the majority in Zimbabwe.

European contact began with Vasco da Gama's voyage to India. He reached modern Mozambique in 1498. Over the next 350 years, the Portuguese gained control of the entire coast. During this time, some slave-trading was carried on, but very little. The main reason the Portuguese wanted the territory was to supply fresh fruit and vegetables to their ships on the long journey from Europe to the Far East.

The Portuguese did not penetrate far inland, except in the Zambezi valley, where they established a trading station at Tete. When the Scramble for Africa began, the Portuguese moved inland all along the coast. They hoped to link Mozambique with Angola and form one great Portuguese empire stretching right across Africa. They did not succeed. The British occupied modern Zimbabwe and Zambia, separating the two Portuguese colonies.

In 1964 an armed rebellion began for independence, led by the Front for the Liberation of Mozambique (Frelimo). In 1975 Frelimo's efforts were finally successful. The country became independent as the People's Republic of Mozambique.

The first flag was of unusual design, four bands of color spreading out from the truck, with an emblem. In 1983 a new flag was adopted. The new design was based on the flag Frelimo had used during the armed struggle. It has stripes of green over black over yellow, separated by white, with a red triangle in the hoist containing a yellow star. On the star are a black rifle and hoe and a white book outlined in black. Green is for agriculture, black for the majority of the people, yellow for mineral wealth and red for the liberation struggle, while white is for non-African minorities. The emblem shows the unity of the peasants, the soldiers and the intellectuals.

NAMIBIA

Namibia is the newest independent state in Africa. It achieved independence on March 21, 1990. It was formerly known as South West Africa.

Namibia is a mainly desert country. It takes its name from the Namib Desert. Although this covers much of the country, there are also areas of fertility, and valuable mineral deposits, especially around Tsumab and Grootfontein.

There are several tribes in the country, the largest of which are the Herero and the Ovambo. These peoples developed a civilization before the whites arrived in the nineteenth century. There are also many desert-dwellers, often known as the Bushmen, but more correctly as the San.

In the 1890's Germany colonized the area. There was resistance, and the Germans had to fight a serious war against the Herero before they could control the territory. During the First World War, South African forces conquered the country and, after the war, it was given to South Africa as a mandate. After World War II, this was changed and South West Africa became a United Nations Trust Territory.

In the 1960's concern arose that South Africa had introduced its system of Apartheid into Namibia, and was ruling it as part of its own territory. An armed struggle began, led by the South West African People's Organization (SWAPO). The U.N. withdrew its approval of South Africa, and announced that SWAPO was the only legitimate representative of the country. Finally, in 1990, South Africa granted independence to Namibia.

The flag is based on that of SWAPO. It has a red diagonal stripe, edged white. The top triangle is blue and has a gold, twelve-rayed sun. The lower triangle is green. The blue is for the sky and the desire for rain in this mostly desert country. The green is for agriculture. The red commemorates the armed struggle, and the gold sun lights the way to the future.

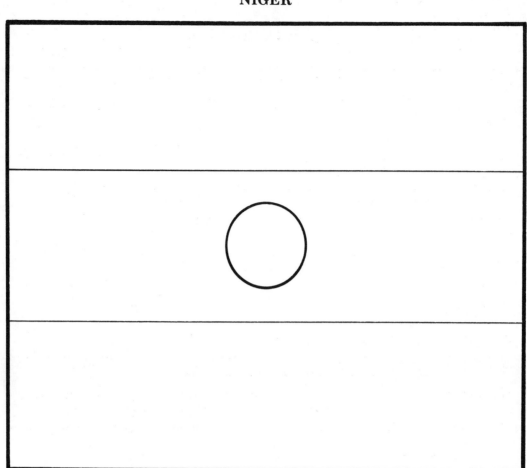

The six million people who live in Niger (pronounced Nee-zhair) are very mixed. The largest group is the Hausa, who also live in Nigeria. There are also Arabs, Berbers, Songhai, Tuareg and Djerma.

The territory of modern Niger was partly within the old Songhai empire. The Arabs, crossing the desert from modern Algeria and Libya, converted the people of the territory to Islam. This is still the strongest religion in Niger.

The first Europeans to visit the country were Germans. Several German explorers crossed Niger in the nineteenth century, but it was the French who took control of the country in 1890. They came from the north, through Algeria, but the first part they controlled in Niger was the south. This was because they rushed south to Zinder and the Niger river, to stop the British who were coming north through modern Nigeria. Where the two groups met became the frontier. This had nothing to do with tribal groups or areas, only with the wish of each country to seize as much land as possible. The result is that there are Hausa and Djerma people in both Niger and Nigeria.

France included Niger in French West Africa. In 1946 a very limited form of self-government was allowed, but independence only came on August 3, 1960. The flag chosen had been adopted in 1959, when it was known that the country would soon be independent.

The flag is a horizontal tricolor of orange over white over green. It has unusual proportions, making it look very short and almost square. The orange stripe is for the desert of the north. White is for awareness of God, for purity and innocence. Green is for the fertile south. The orange circle represents the sun, and the spirit of sacrifice of the people of Niger for the common good. Unfortunately, since independence there has been a steady move southward of the Sahara desert. This had made more and more of Niger infertile every year, so that now there is constant danger of famine.

NIGERIA

More than 90 million people live in Nigeria, making it the most heavily populated country in the continent. One fifth of the entire population of Africa live in Nigeria. They belong to over 250 different tribes. The largest tribes are the Hausa of the north, the Yoruba of the west and the Ibo of the south-east.

Between 1849 and 1861, British ships patrolled the coastal areas to stop the slave-trade. At times they established small bases. The occupation of Lagos as a permanent base in 1861 was the beginning of British colonization and of modern Nigeria. From this tiny foothold, British control was extended along the coast, and the Oil Rivers Protectorate was established.

The center and north came under British rule later, during the Scramble. George Goldie gained control of much of the Niger river and played a part somewhat similar to that of Cecil Rhodes in southern Africa. The British governor, Frederick Lugard, developed a system of governing colonies which was later applied in most British territories.

On October 1, 1960, Nigeria became independent as a federation of three regions. Three years later, on the same date, the country became a republic. Unfortunately, tribal divisions arose and became very bitter. In 1967 the Eastern Region, inhabited mostly by Ibos, tried to break away and form itself into a separate country. The result was a bitter civil war until 1970. Unity has since been restored.

The flag of Nigeria is a simple tribar of green, white, green. It was the result of a competition, in which there were more than 3,000 entries. The winning entry showed the present flag with a red sun on the white stripe. The sun was omitted by the committee which judged the competition. Green is for agriculture, the main natural resource of the country. White is for peace and national unity.

RWANDA

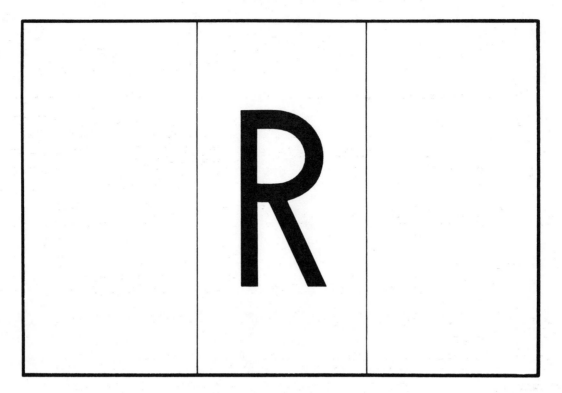

Rwanda is a very small country in area, but it has a comparatively large population. It is only one-fiftieth the size of Chad, for example, but has more people than Chad.

The story of Rwanda is almost the same as that of Burundi. Rwanda has the same main tribal groups, Tutsi and Bahutu. The first colonial rulers were the Germans. They occupied both countries in 1889 and ruled them as German East Africa, together with the mainland part of modern Tanzania. After World War I Rwanda, together with Burundi, was given to Belgium as a mandate called Ruanda-Urundi. At the end of World War II, the mandate was changed so that the country became a United Nations Trust Territory, which was almost the same thing.

The tribal rulers of Rwanda had always been the Tutsi. In 1959, while the country was still a Trust Territory, the Bahutu rose against the Tutsi. Many of the Tutsi were killed and over 150,000 fled to neighboring countries. The violence was so great that the Belgian authorities were unable to stop it. Partly because of this, Rwanda did not get independence at the same time as the Belgian Congo (now Zaïre).

In 1962, the United Nations decided to give independence to both Burundi and Rwanda. Unlike Burundi, which began as a kingdom, Rwanda was a republic from the beginning.

The Rwanda flag is a vertical tricolor of red, yellow and green, with a large black "R" on the center stripe. Without the "R" the flag would be identical with that of Guinea. The "R" is for the name of the country, but it has also been understood to mean "Revolution" (by the Bahutu against the Tutsi), "Referendum" (which in 1961 decided on independence) and "Republic". The red is for the bloodshed before independence, yellow is for peace, tranquility and liberation, while green is for hope and agriculture. Black shows an African country and solidarity with other African states.

SÃO TOMÉ E PRINCIPE

This country has one of the smallest populations of any member of the O.A.U., only about 100,000. The people are mostly African and mixed African-Portuguese. The country consists of two islands, situated off the coast of Equatorial Guinea and Gabon.

The Portuguese explorers reported the islands to their king in the fifteenth century. At that time the islands were uninhabited. In 1493 the Portuguese made their first settlement on São Tomé. At first, this was only a supply-base for other explorers (and later for ships passing between Europe and India). In 1522, São Tomé was taken under the administration of the Portuguese king. Principe followed soon after. The slave-trade became the most important business of the islands. Almost every inhabitant of the country today is a descendant of slaves, slave-traders or both. The islands remained under Portuguese rule for 450 years.

When rebellions for independence began in the Portuguese colonies, there were also attempts in São Tomé and Principe. These were not as wide-spread as the risings in the others. This was because the islands were so small, it was easy for the Portuguese to keep control.

In 1975, the people were asked whether they wished to be independent or to remain under Portuguese rule. They voted for independence, and on June 12, 1975 the islands became a republic. A new national flag was adopted on November 5 of that year. The flag was based on that of the Movement for the Liberation of São Tomé e Principe.

The flag shows a broad yellow band between two narrower green stripes. The green is for the vegetation of the islands and for agriculture. Yellow is for the sun and for cacao, the most important product of the country. The red triangle is for those who were killed in the struggle, and for unity and independence. The two stars are for the two islands which make up the country, and are black to show the country's association with Africa.

SENEGAL

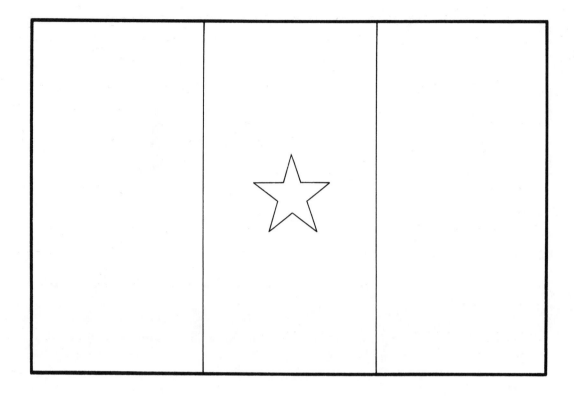

Senegal is situated at the westernmost point of Africa. The population is almost entirely black, but there are also a few Arabs. Senegal formed part of the ancient Ghana and Mali empires. Many of the people were converted to Islam, but not all, as happened in other areas.

The earliest contact with Europeans was in 1364. Normans from France established a trading settlement in the area. It did not last long. The Portuguese did not show much interest, as they wanted to press on quickly to India. Then in the fifteenth century, the French began to trade in the country. In 1658 France established the town of St. Louis. This was not named for a French saint, but for the first Senegalese saint, St. Louis de Senegal. Unfortunately, St. Louis soon developed into the main French slave-trading port. In 1854, the French captured Dakar and began to extend their power inland. By 1865 all of modern Senegal was in their hands.

Dakar was the capital of French West Africa, of which Senegal was part. It was in Senegal that the French began their experiment of allowing colonies to elect representatives to the French Assembly in Paris. They began with just four towns in Senegal. Later this practice extended over most of the French colonies.

In 1959 Senegal joined with French Sudan in the Mali Federation. Little more than a year later, Senegal broke away from it. French Sudan became Mali and Senegal re-adopted her old name. The first president was Léopold Senghor, a noted poet in France, and a former minister in the French Government.

Senegal adopted the flag of the Federation, a vertical tricolor of green, yellow and red, with a green star added. Green is for agriculture, yellow for purity and natural resources, red for courage and the struggle for independence. The three colors are also those of the main Senegalese political parties. The green star is for the idea of unity of peoples and African freedom.

SEYCHELLES

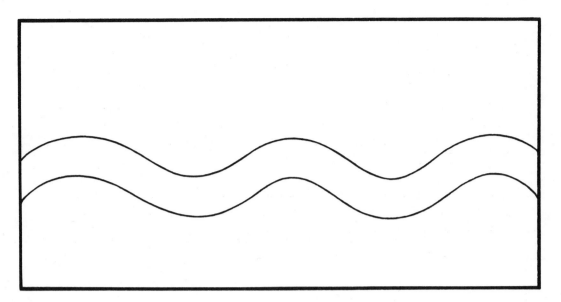

Seychelles consists of eighty-seven islands in the Indian Ocean. The population is a mixture of African, Malay, Indian and French elements. Apart from the Seychelles islands themselves, the country also includes the Des Roches, Aldabra and Farquhar islands. Yet the population is only 70,000, the smallest of any O.A.U. member.

When the Portuguese explorer, Vasco da Gama, discovered the islands in 1502, they were uninhabited. They remained so until the French began to colonize them in 1742. In 1756, the French took control in the name of King Louis XV, and named them for the then French Minister of Finance (who had found the money to pay for the colonization). The French started plantations on the islands, and imported African slaves to work on them.

The British captured the islands in 1794, and they became officially British in 1814. Britain then ruled them until they achieved independence in 1976. The British introduced the Malay and Indian elements of the population, but these were not brought as slaves.

On June 29, 1976 Seychelles became an independent state, and adopted a flag of red, white and blue, somewhat like the flag of Burundi without the central circle. This flag honored the British and French traditions and cultural background of the country. Less than a year later, a revolution overthrew the first independent government and tore down the flag.

The new flag raised on June 25, 1977 and adopted officially on September 5 of the same year, has red at the top and green at the bottom, separated by a wavy white stripe. It is based very closely on the flag of the United People's Party which carried out the revolution. Red is for revolution and progress, green for the land and for natural resources, white for the coasts and the riches of the ocean. The form of the white stripe recalls the waves of the sea. Only two other countries have wavy stripes on their flags. One is the British Indian Ocean Territory, an island group near Seychelles. The other is Kiribati, also an island country, but in the Pacific Ocean.

SIERRA LEONE

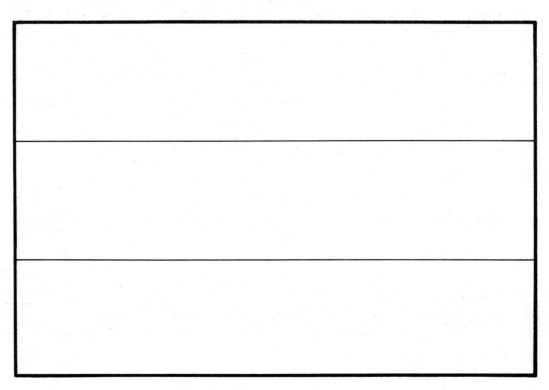

The name "Sierra Leone" means "Mountains of the Lions". The name was given by the Portuguese explorer, Pedro de Cintra. He explored the coast of the country in 1462 and noticed frequent thunderstorms over the coastal mountains. From a distance, the thunder sounded like the roaring of lions.

The first European traders were interested only in slaves. Sierra Leone was a major center of the trade for 200 years. It was on the coast of Sierra Leone that the slave-trader, John Newton, experienced a religious conversion. It turned him against the slave-trade and made him preach against it. It was also the origin of his song "Amazing Grace." Partly as a result of Newton's preaching, William Wilberforce formed the Anti-Slavery Society. It also caused the British to take control of the country in 1808, to use as a base for their ships which were engaged in suppressing the trade.

In 1788, even before taking control of the coast, the British had founded Freetown, today the country's capital. This was settled by freed slaves, much as Liberia was founded by the American Colonization Society. Again this was the result of Newton's preaching. It also explains why so many people in Sierra Leone have English names. They are the descendants of the freed slaves. By 1896, Britain had established a protectorate over the inland areas, and the entire territory of modern Sierra Leone was under British rule.

On April 26, 1961, Sierra Leone achieved independence. The flag adopted is of simple design, a horizontal tricolor of green over white over blue. It was the winning entry in a competition. Green is for vegetation and the fertility of the farmlands. White is for peace and justice. Blue is for the ocean.

SOMALIA

Somalia takes its name from the Somali people. Traditionally they are nomads, but this is slowly changing into a more settled way of life. Although there was no formal state or central government of the Somalis, they were a distinct, united group before the colonial period.

The first newcomers were not Europeans, but Ethiopians. The Ethiopian emperors Theodore and Menelik tried to extend their control into Somali areas. Then came the Europeans. France, Italy and Britain all tried to gain control. In 1884, Britain began a settlement on the northern coast, and established a protectorate there in 1887. Two years later, Italy began the occupation of the east coast. Italy enlarged her control to its greatest extent in 1924.

After World War II, the United Nations allowed Italy to administer Italian Somaliland for ten years from 1950, after which it was to be independent. The territory became independent in 1960, and united with British Somaliland, which became independent at the same time. The two together form Somalia. This does not include Somali groups in Djibouti, Ethiopia and Kenya, all of whom are claimed by Somalia.

Somalia clashed with Kenya over disputed areas, and fought a major war with Ethiopia for the same reason. Somalia lost when Cuba and the USSR supported Ethiopia. After that, Somalia became an ally of the United States.

The flag is light blue with a white star, the colors of the United Nations, which sponsored Somalia's independence. The five points of the star are for the former Italian and British Somaliland, and Somali-inhabited territories in Djibouti, Kenya and Ethiopia, still claimed by Somalia.

In 1991 a coup overthrew the Somali government, but led to civil war. All government collapsed. Former British Somaliland tried to secede. Armies, tribes and clans fought among themselves and famine ravaged the country. In 1992 American and French forces entered the country to protect and distribute food supplies to starving people. They have had to fight to do this, and the terrible plight of the people of Somalia continues.

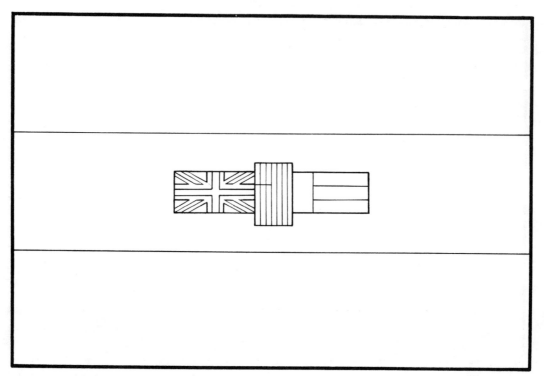

The first people in South Africa were the San and the Khoi, both primitive peoples. The Bantu began to move into the country from the north in the seventeenth century. There were many tribes and they moved south slowly, pushing the San and Khoi ahead of them.

The Portuguese passed the tip of Africa in 1487, but the first white settlers were the Dutch. In 1652 they built a fort at the Cape, with a garden to supply food to passing ships. They spread inland, and met the Bantu coming south 140 years later.

In 1815 the British took control of the Cape. The Dutch disliked British rule. Almost all of them were farmers and they could not keep their Coloured and Malay slaves. In the 1830s, many Dutch left the Cape and went north in the Great Trek. They established two republics, the Orange Free State and the Transvaal. They were known as Boers, from the Dutch word for farmer. Between 1899 and 1902 there was war between Britain and the republics. Britain won, and in 1910 set up the Union of South Africa, a union of the British colonies of Natal and the Cape, with the former republics.

In 1948 the National Party became the government and has remained so ever since. The National Party introduced apartheid, separating the various peoples by race, and allowing only whites to vote. In 1961, South Africa was made a republic. South Africa has given a form of independence to five of its Black areas, known as Bantustans, but only South Africa recognizes them.

The flag is based on the first Dutch flag to fly over South Africa, a horizontal tricolor of orange over white over blue. In the center is the British flag, with blue triangles and red vertical and diagonal crosses edged in white. The central flag of the Orange Free State has four white and three orange stripes, with a canton of red, white and blue (from left to right as seen here). The other flag is that of the Transvaal. It has a vertical green band and horizontal red, white, and blue stripes. So the flag shows the union of the British colonies and Boer republics.

Recently the South African government decided to abandon apartheid and create a non-racial, democratic state. Negotiations continue, but there is still a long way to go, and divisions have emerged in the black communities, often bringing violence between them. Future developments are at best uncertain.

SUDAN

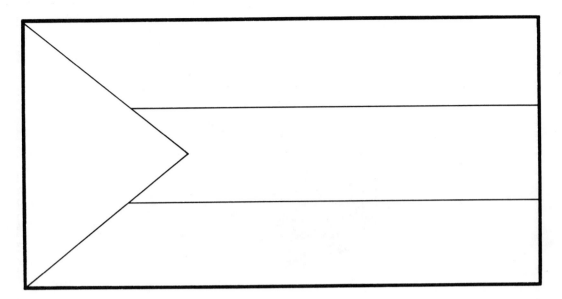

The Sudan was at one time part of the Egyptian empire. The Sudanese, then called Nubians, conquered Egypt for about 100 years. From the sixth century on a Coptic Christian civilization flourished in The Sudan. Later, by the fifteenth century, the Arabs converted the people of the Sudan to Islam.

The people of Sudan were always divided between the Arabs of the north and the Nilotic or black peoples of the south. Their first real unity came in the early nineteenth century, when Mehemet Ali, ruler of Egypt, conquered the territory. When the British occupied Egypt in 1882, they began to penetrate up the Nile valley. There they came into the then independent Sudan state. At the same time, French troops entered the country from the west. Britain and France were almost ready to go to war over the country. Then the French government realized that if they fought Britain, they would lose. In addition they wanted British friendship, to support them in their quarrel with Germany. In 1898 the French withdrew. Britain established a condominium over the Sudan with Egypt. This meant that both Britain and Egypt ruled the country.

In 1922 Egypt became independent. Although the name Anglo-Egyptian Sudan was kept, Britain soon exercised complete control. This lasted until January 1, 1956, when the Sudan became an independent republic.

The first flag of Sudan was a horizontal tricolor of blue, yellow and green. The colors were for the blue waters of the Nile, flowing over the sands of the desert and turning them into agricultural land. The new flag was adopted in 1970, after a revolution. It has horizontal stripes of red, white and black, with a green triangle. It is based on the flag of Egypt, and contains the Arab Nationalist colors, symbolizing the four historic ruling families of Islam. Red is for the Hashemites, white for the Ummayyads, black for the Abbassids and green for the Fatimids. The colors can also have other meanings. Red is for the blood of Arab heroes and white for the purity of the Muslim faith and the Arab cause. Black is for the fate of the enemies of the Arabs and for the "dark past" before Islam, while green is for Islam itself, as it was the favorite color of the Prophet Muhammad.

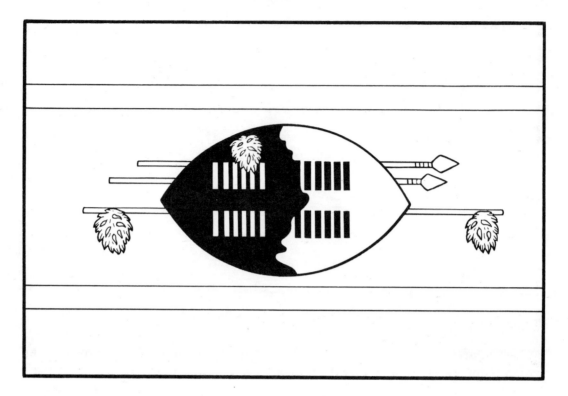

Swaziland lies between Mozambique and South Africa. The Swazi people are of Nguni origin. They settled north of the Pongolo river in the late 18th century, at about the same time that Shaka was founding the Zulu kingdom in modern Natal. In 1820, Zulus prevented the Swazi from spreading southward and drove them back into the mountains after a very bloody defeat.

The Swazi king, Sobhuza I, established a kingdom which covered almost exactly the same territory as the present state. His successor, King Mswati, ruled from 1836 to 1868. He organized the kingdom and established a permanent army.

After Mswati's death. Swaziland found itself in a difficult situation. The Portuguese were pushing inland from modern Maputo and threatening to enter Swazi territory. In the west was the Boer republic of the Transvaal, not seeking colonies, but wanting to secure its eastern frontier in the Swazi mountains. In the south were the British, who had just beaten the mighty Zulu kingdom. It looked as though Swaziland was doomed to lose its independence to one or another of these. Britain promised to respect Swazi independence, and other countries would not go against Britain at first. Then in 1882, the Boers defeated the British at the battle of Majuba. When the British were no longer able to protect Swaziland, it became a protectorate of the Transvaal.

With the defeat of the Boer states by Britain in 1902, Swaziland became a British protectorate. The only difference was that Britain now ran Swaziland's foreign affairs. Neither the Boers nor the British interfered with the king or with the way the country's internal affairs were conducted. In 1968 Swaziland regained independence as a kingdom.

The broad red stripe on the flag is for courage. On it appear a black and white Swazi war-shield and weapons, to recall the history of the country. The narrow yellow stripes are for prosperity and the blue edges for the sky and for rain. The feather tufts are blue, with small red decorations. The Swazi Royal Standard, the king's personal flag, adds a yellow lion in the center of the top blue stripe.

TANZANIA

The oldest human remains ever found were at Olduvai Gorge in Tanzania. This means that Tanzania is probably one of the cradles of humanity. There are several tribes in modern Tanzania, which is a union of mainland Tanganyika and the island of Zanzibar.

Portuguese explorers and traders visited the coast from the late fifteenth century, but the Arabs had traded along the coast for centuries before the Europeans came. One of their largest bases for slave-trading was on the island of Zanzibar. The name of the island is a form of Arabic words meaning the "coast of the black people."

Beginning in 1884, Germany established a protectorate over the coast, which expanded inland until it reached Lake Tanganyika. This protectorate included Burundi and Rwanda, as well as modern mainland Tanzania. During World War I, German forces in Tanganyika, both white and black, under General von Lettow-Vorbeck, carried out a brilliant guerilla campaign, lasting over four years. Von Lettow surrendered only after the war had ended in Europe.

Britain gained control of Zanzibar in 1895, in order to end the Arab slave-trade. It later became a base for Allied troops fighting against the Germans under von Lettow.

Tanganyika became a British Mandate in 1919. In 1961 it gained independence and adopted a horizontal tribar of green, black and green, separated by yellow. In 1963, Zanzibar became independent and chose a red flag with a green circle and two yellow cloves. A month later, after a revolution, the new government adopted a flag of green, black and blue stripes.

In 1964, soon after the Zanzibari revolution, Tanganyika and Zanzibar united to form Tanzania. The new flag combined the former flags. The wide black diagonal stripe is for the people. It is edged yellow for mineral wealth. The upper triangle is green, for the land, and the lower triangle is blue for the sea.

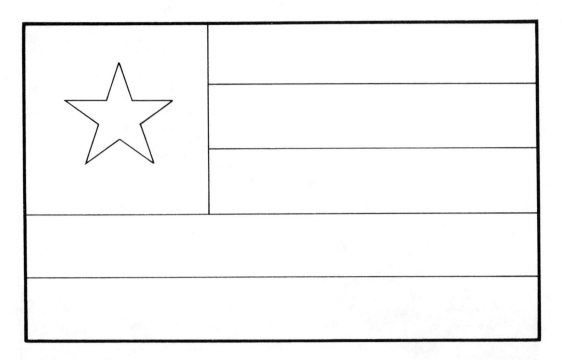

There are thirteen main tribes in Togo, which lies between Ghana and Benin. The people in the south are of Bantu origin, while those in the north are Hamitic. There has been a tradition of rivalry between the two groups.

Portuguese explorers visited the coast of Togo, and later there were a few other European trading settlements. Happily, none of these was to do with the slave-trade, and hardly any people from modern Togo were either involved in the trade or victims of it.

During the Scramble for Africa, Togo came under German control and was known as Togoland. At that time it was larger than it is today, as it included part of modern Ghana. In 1919 the German colony was divided under mandate. 40 percent was given to Britain and 60 percent to France. It is the part given to France which forms the modern state of Togo.

Before independence, Togo used a flag which had the French tricolor in the canton and two yellow stars on green. This showed the desire that the two parts of former Togoland would one day be reunited. It was not to be. When Ghana achieved independence, the people in the part of former Togoland which had been given to Britain were asked if they wanted to join Togo, or to become independent with the rest of Ghana. They chose to stay with Ghana.

On April 27, 1960, Togo became an independent republic. At once it adopted its present flag, based on the flag it had used before independence. The stars became two yellow stripes on green, and two of the colors of the French tricolor remained in the canton, but changed from stripes into a white star on a red square.

The colors each have two meanings. Green is for agriculture and hope for the future. Yellow is for work and for Togo's mineral resources. Red is for charity and fidelity and for respect for all human beings. White is for purity and wisdom and honors national independence.

TUNISIA

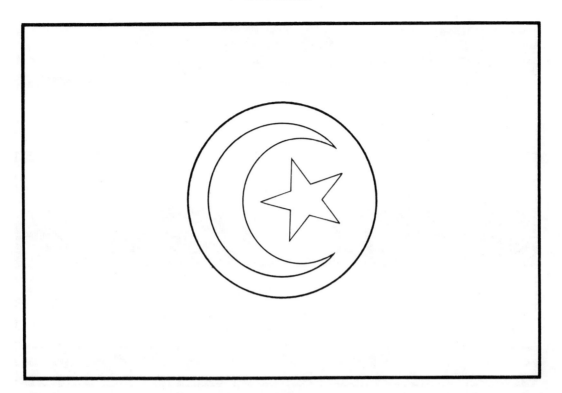

3000 years ago, merchants from the Middle East founded a city on the north coast of Africa. This was Carthage. It grew to control most of north Africa, Spain and parts of Italy. It fought three wars with Rome, in one of which the great general Hannibal was involved. Rome finally won and destroyed Carthage. The country became part of the Roman Empire.

In the seventh century Muslim Arabs made the territory a military headquarters. They built a fort, Kairouan, and a port, Tunis, from which the modern country takes its name. After being conquered by the Almohads from modern Algeria, Tunisia was again briefly independent before falling under the control of the Ottoman Empire in 1574.

When the Ottoman Empire became weak in the nineteenth century, France and Italy both wanted to take Tunis. France seized it in 1881. This put Tunisia under yet another foreign ruler until 1956. This does not mean that all was quiet. There were several rebellions against France, and for most of the time, France had to keep strong military forces in the country.

On March 20, 1956, Tunisia achieved independence. It was ruled by the Bey, a traditional ruler, whose title had existed for centuries. This Bey was not popular, as many believed that he had been too ready to cooperate with the French. A year later he was overthrown and a republic was declared, with Habib Bourguiba as president.

The flag of Tunisia is much older than independence. It may be based on the flag of the Ottoman Empire, modern Turkey, which is red, with a white crescent and star. It is also true that Tunis used red and white flags before the Ottomans ruled the country. Certainly the present flag has been in use continuously since about 1835. This makes it the oldest flag in Africa. The red crescent and star show a Muslim state. They are on a white circle for unity. The circle is on a red field for the blood shed by those who fought for freedom. These are modern meanings given to an old flag.

UGANDA

Uganda was once called the "Pearl of Africa." This name is not now used. Long years of oppression, war, banditry and drought have almost ruined what is potentially one of the richest countries in Africa. There are many tribes and languages in Uganda. Radio Uganda broadcasts in no less than ten African languages, as well as in English.

The first Europeans visited the country in 1862. They were a British expedition searching for the source of the Nile. Ten years later there were Christian missionaries, again mainly British, living and working in the country. In 1893, Britain established a protectorate over Buganda, one of the areas which make up modern Uganda, and comprising about half the modern country. One reason for this was to protect the missionaries. Gradually the remaining areas came under British rule until, by 1903, all of modern Uganda was under the protectorate. One of the early British administrators was Frederick Lugard, who also worked in Nigeria.

Independence was somewhat delayed by tribal quarrels. It finally came on October 9, 1962, and Uganda became a republic in 1967. The first president was the king of Buganda, Sir Frederick Mutesa II. He was overthrown in a bloody coup by the Prime Minister, Milton Obote. Obote was in turn overthrown by Idi Amin, who had an eight-year reign of terror until Ugandan exiles and Tanzanian troops overthrew him in 1979. After several coups, Obote resumed the presidency, then quickly showed he was as bad as Amin, and he was again overthrown. The new president, Musevene, has greatly improved matters, but Uganda is still very unstable.

The flag has horizontal stripes of black over yellow over red, repeated to make a unique design. Black is for the people, yellow for the sun and red for brotherhood. Originally red stood for the blood shed for freedom, but as so much was shed later, the meaning was changed. In the center white circle is a crowned crane, Uganda's national bird, which appeared on the colonial flag. It is black and grey in color, with a yellow crest, red tail feathers and red patch under the beak.

ZAÏRE

Zaïre is the third largest country in Africa after Sudan and Algeria. There are hundreds of different tribes in the country.

In 1482 the Portuguese explorer, Diogo Cão, visited the mouth of the Congo river and erected there a stone cross, claiming the area for Portugal. In fact the claim was not followed by colonization.

In the nineteenth century the American explorer, Stanley, told the world about the basin of the Congo river and aroused interest in it. Suddenly several countries claimed the area. At the Berlin Colonial Conference of 1885, it was agreed that no country's claim was correct. To stop the various countries from taking over anyway, the Conference asked King Leopold of Belgium to rule it as the Congo Free State. This left the country independent (even if with a European ruler). As Belgium was a very small country, the larger states would not be jealous. King Leopold started a company to trade in the area. For over twenty years he ruled the country as if it were his private property. By 1908, most people in Europe knew that Leopold's agents in the Congo had been guilty of horrible atrocities against the people. Leopold handed over control to the Belgian government.

The country remained under Belgian rule as the Belgian Congo until 1960. On June 30, 1960 it was given independence. There was almost no preparation for independence. All parties were tribally or regionally based. None was national. No blacks had been trained for administration. Almost at once the country collapsed into civil war, coups and revolts. Tribalism and separatism were everywhere. Even when General Mobutu took over in 1965, it was a long time before stability returned.

The present flag is the third since independence. The first two were based on an old flag used 1885-1908. The present design is from 1971, when the country was renamed Zaïre. It is green for forests and agriculture. The yellow disc shows the sun. The brown arm holds the torch of freedom (brown outlines, yellow pattern), which has red flames.

ZAMBIA

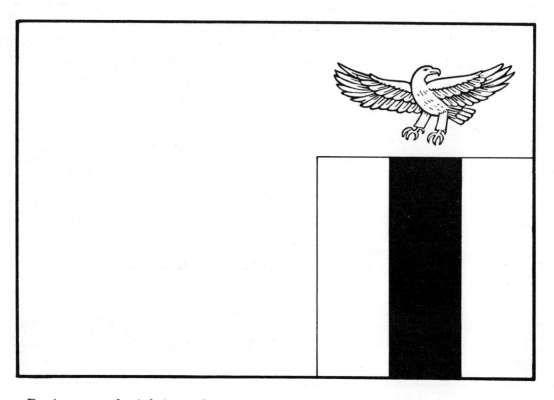

During pre-colonial times the area of modern Zambia was part of a great trans-African trade route. Parts of the ancient Luba and Lunda kingdoms are included in the country's present frontiers. Zambia was affected the Nguni expansion of the early nineteenth century. In particular the forces led by Sebitwane and Zwangendaba passed through the territory.

In 1851, David Livingstone, the missionary and explorer, travelled along the Zambesi river on the Zambian bank. Years later, on another journey, he died at a village in eastern Zambia. The Zambian city of Livingstone on the Zambesi is named for him.

In the 1890's Zambia came under British rule, as a result of the work of Cecil Rhodes. At this time, Portugal was trying to link Angola and Mozambique through modern Zambia. At another time, Germany tried to link German East Africa (modern mainland Tanzania) with German South-West Africa (modern Namibia), also through Zambia. At first Zambia was part of the territory known as Rhodesia. In 1910 that territory was divided into Northern Rhodesia and Southern Rhodesia. Northern Rhodesia was a protectorate, while Southern Rhodesia was a colony.

In 1953, Northern and Southern Rhodesia and Nyasaland (now Malawi) were joined in a federation by Britain. From the beginning, African political opinion was against federation. At the end of 1963, the federation came to an end.

On October 24, 1964, Northern Rhodesia became independent as the Republic of Zambia. It was the first former British colony to achieve independence directly as a republic. On that date it raised its new flag. This was based on the party flag of the United National Independence Party (U.N.I.P.), which had become the government. The flag has a unique design. The green field is for agriculture. The vertical bars are red, black and orange, from center to fly. Red is for the blood shed for freedom, black for the majority of the people and orange for mineral wealth. The orange eagle stands for Zambia's freedom and for the country's ability to rise above its problems.

ZIMBABWE

Great Zimbabwe was the center of a wide-ranging and powerful African civilization. After the Zimbabwe civilization declined, new civilizations arose under the Mwenemutapa and Rozwi. All these were Shona-language cultures. In the 1830's the Matabele arrived from the south. They were part of the Nguni expansion and settled in the west. Soon the Matabele king claimed control of the whole country.

In 1890 European settlers arrived, sent by Cecil Rhodes, with the agreement of King Lobengula of the Matabele. When it was clear that these settlers meant to stay, war broke out in 1893. The Matabele were defeated by the whites and all modern Zimbabwe was under white control. In 1896 occurred the first rebellions against colonialism. The Matabele and Shona both tried to expel the whites but failed.

The country, then known as Rhodesia, was divided into Northern Rhodesia (now Zambia) and Southern Rhodesia (now Zimbabwe) in 1910. In 1953 they were brought together again, with Nyasaland (now Malawi) in a federation. Largely as a result of African opposition to it, federation was dissolved at the end of 1963. With the independence of Zambia in 1964, the white government of Southern Rhodesia changed the name to simply Rhodesia. In 1965 the minority government declared Rhodesia's independence unilaterally. No other country recognized this action.

The armed revolt against white rule began in 1966, but only became nationwide in 1972. By the end of 1979, the whites negotiated with the guerilla forces. Zimbabwe became independent on April 18, 1980.

The Flag of Zimbabwe is based on that of the Zimbabwe African National Union (Patriotic Front) or Z.A.N.U (P.F.), which won the independence election. The stripes from top to bottom are green, yellow, red, black, red, yellow, green. Black is for the majority of the people, red for the blood shed for freedom, yellow and green for mineral and agricultural wealth. The white triangle, edged black, is for unity. The red star is for socialism and internationalism. The gold Zimbabwe Bird is the national emblem, taken from the ancient Zimbabwe civilization.

GLOSSARY OF TERMS

Barracoons: Enclosures to hold slaves until the traders were ready to ship them away from Africa. At first they were simply wooden cages, but later they became permanent stone buildings, including offices.

Byzantine Empire: An empire which ruled much of the Middle East, North Africa and south-eastern Europe. It was centered on Constantinople (known in ancient times as Byzantium, and today as Istanbul) and lasted from the fifth century A.D. to 1453.

Carthaginian Empire: An ancient empire, centered on the city of Carthage (near modern Tunis). It ruled much of North Africa, Spain, Sicily, Sardinia and Corsica until defeated by Rome in the third century B.C.

Circassian: People from the Caucasus mountains in the modern U.S.S.R. They became Muslim, unlike most other peoples from that area.

Coat of arms: This is an official emblem of a country. It is often a design showing the history and culture of the country symbolically. The word comes from the time when knights in armour wore designs on cloth coverings, so that they could be identified.

Islam: The third monotheistic religion after Judaism and Christianity. It was founded by the Prophet Muhammad in the seventh century in Arabia.

Kurdish: Belonging to a people who are now divided between Turkey, Iran and Iraq. They are a very ancient people, but in modern times have never had a state of their own.

Muslim: A believer in Islam. Such people are often wrongly called Mohammedans. This word is utterly wrong and should never be used.

Protectorate: A form of colonialism in which the colonial power took control of a territory in international law, but, while ruling the country and providing services such as posts and police, interfered little with the traditional way of life of the people. In a protectorate, the colonial powers ruled with the help of the chiefs.

Referendum: A vote on an important matter rather than for a government. It could be on the type of government, such as kingdom or republic, or whether a country should be independent or not. Sometimes it has been used to decide to which country a territory should belong.

Scramble for Africa: The period near the end of the nineteenth century when many European countries tried to obtain colonies in Africa, and when most of Africa came under colonial rule.

Vandal: The Vandals were a central European people who invaded the Roman empire in the fourth and fifth centuries A.D. After attacking Rome itself, they moved to Spain and then North Africa, where they set up a kingdom covering much of modern Algeria, Tunisia, Morocco, Sicily and Sardinia. The Vandal kingdom lasted about 100 years, then came under the rule of the Byzantine empire.